Around the World Doodle Book

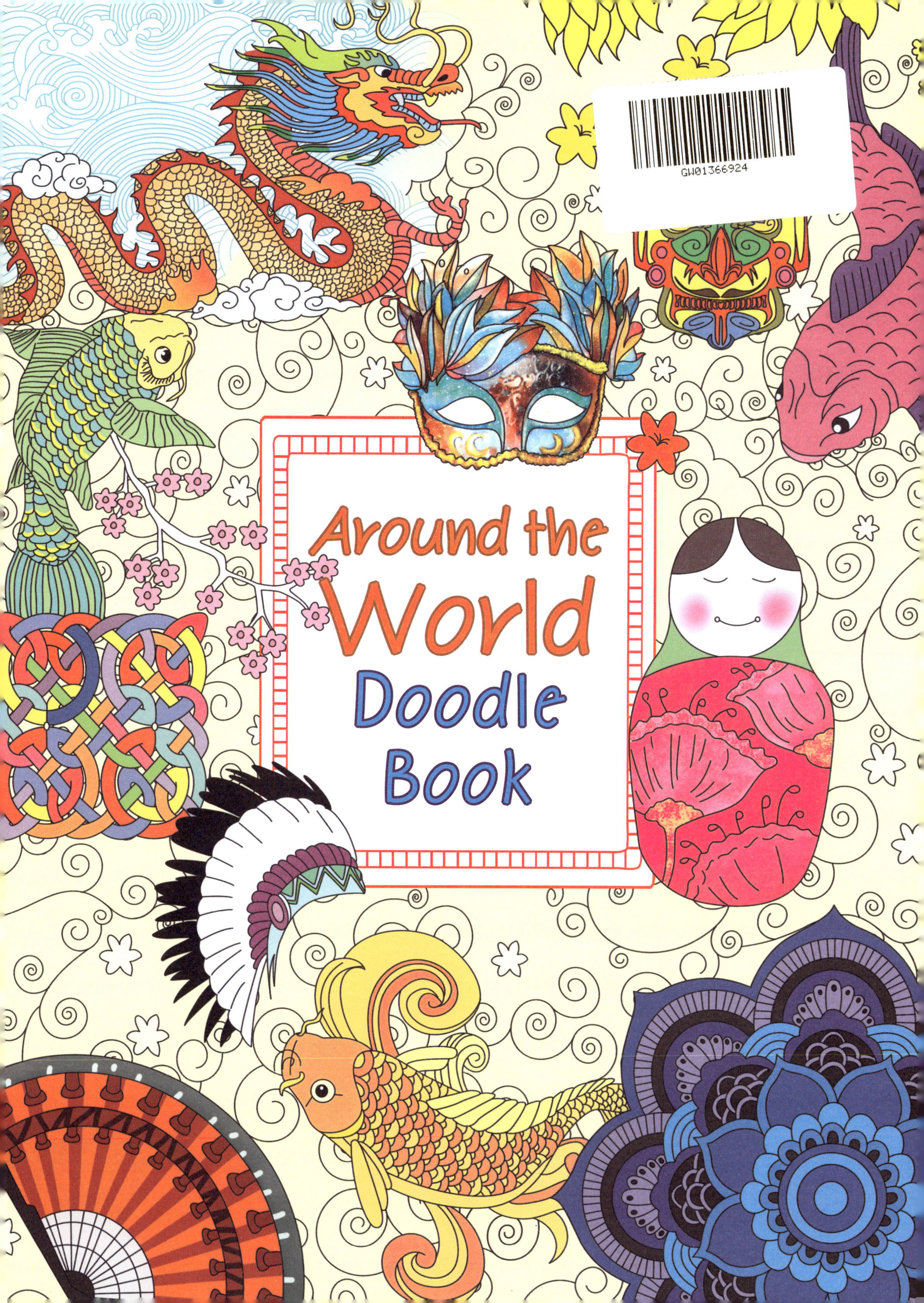

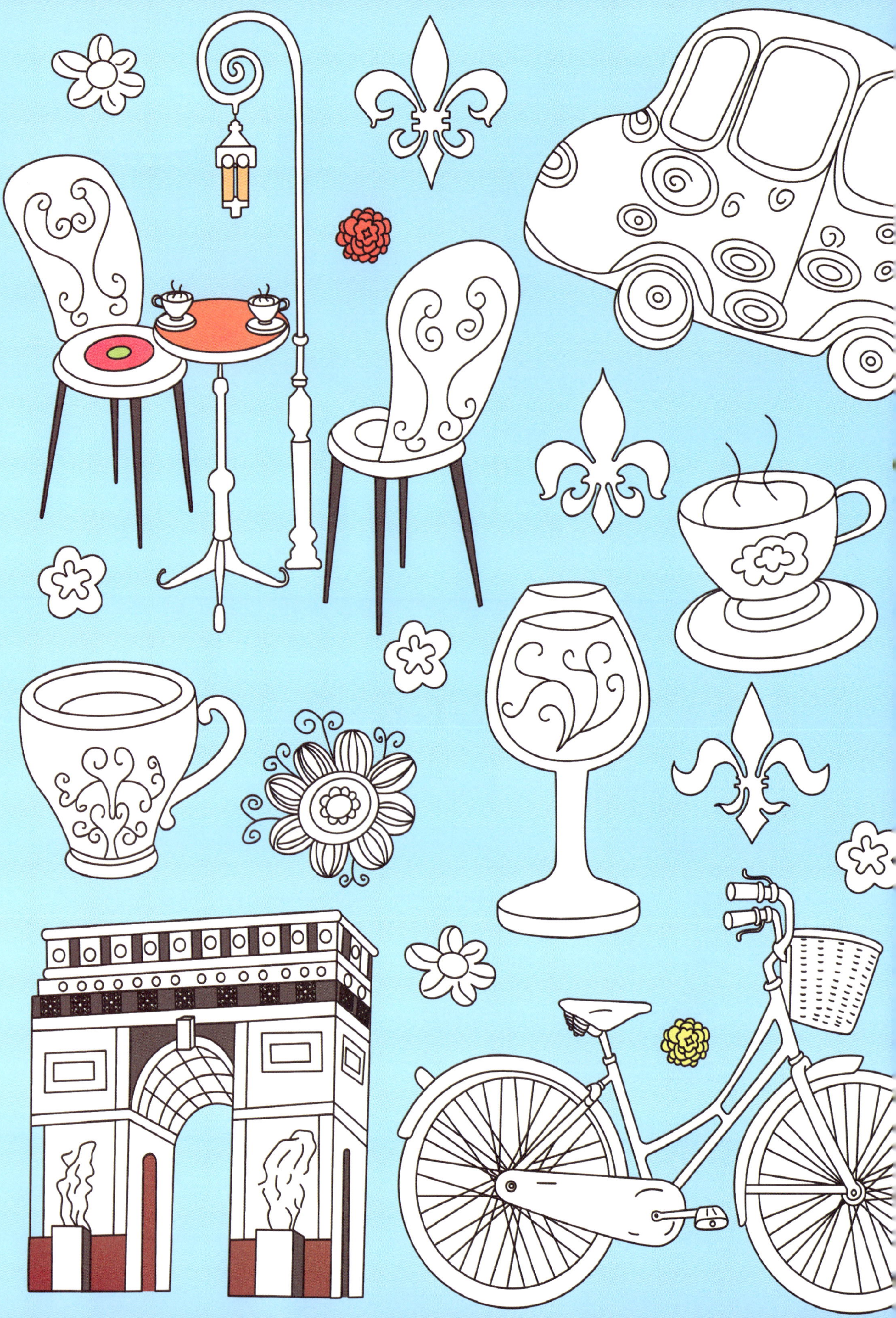

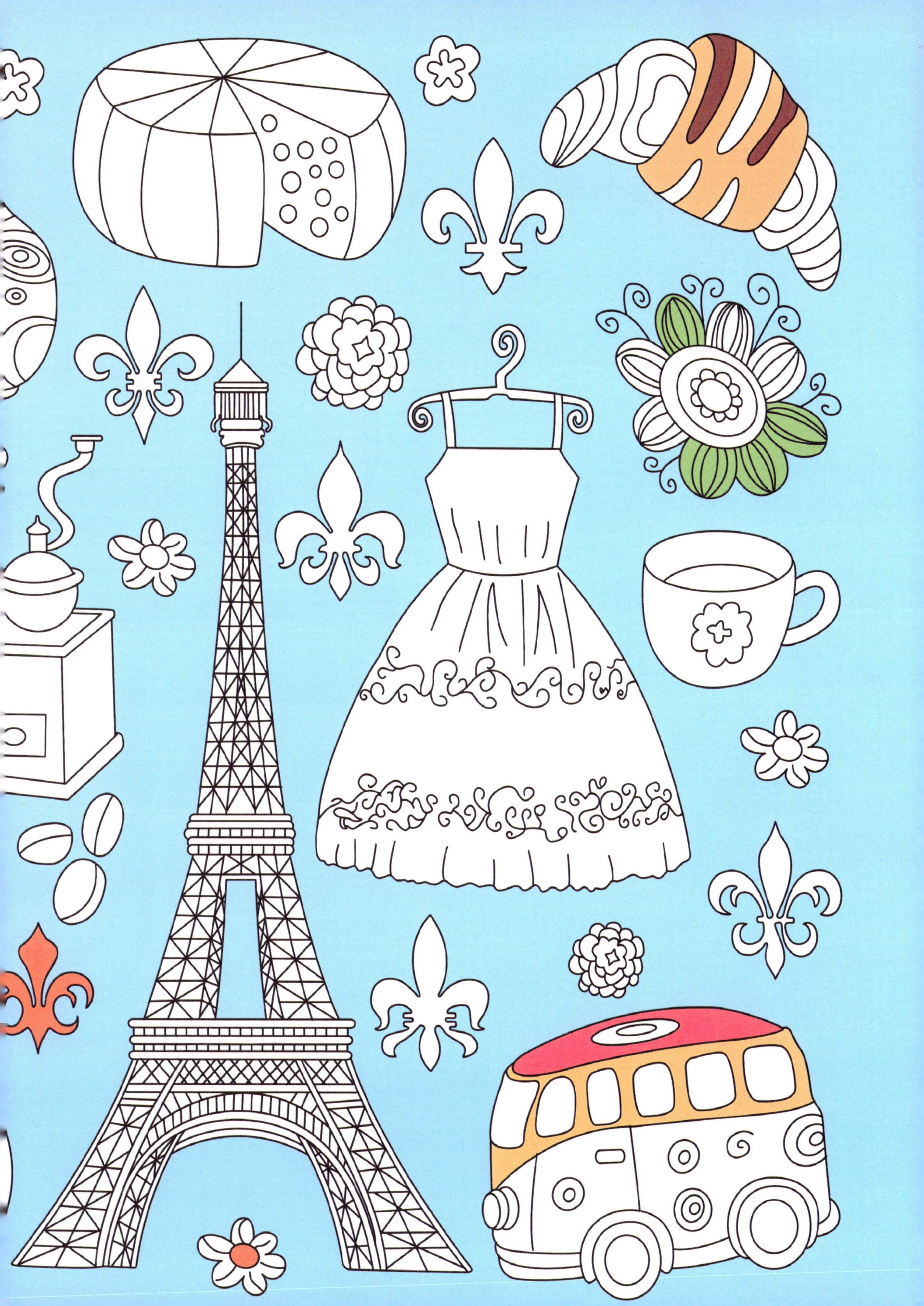

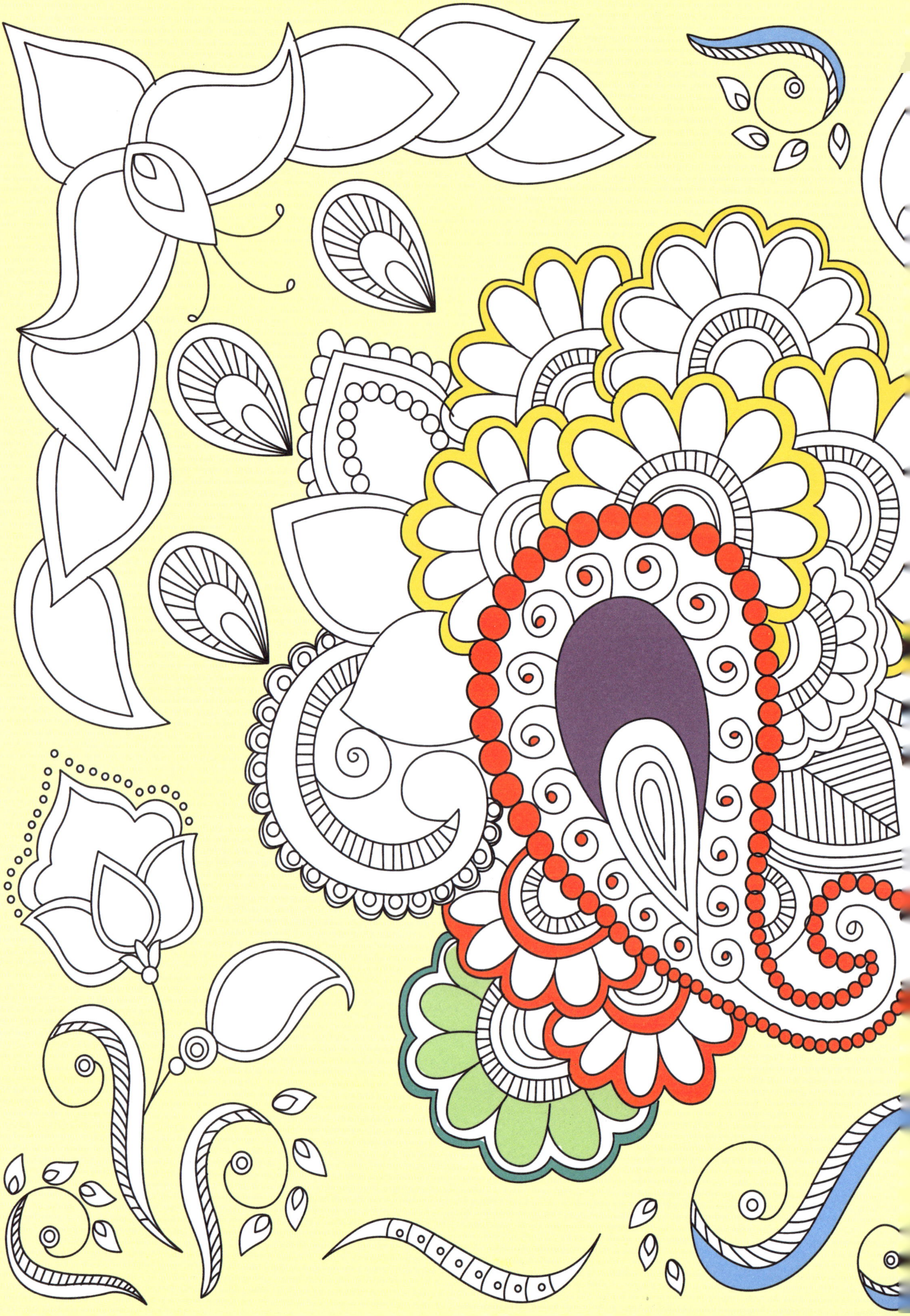

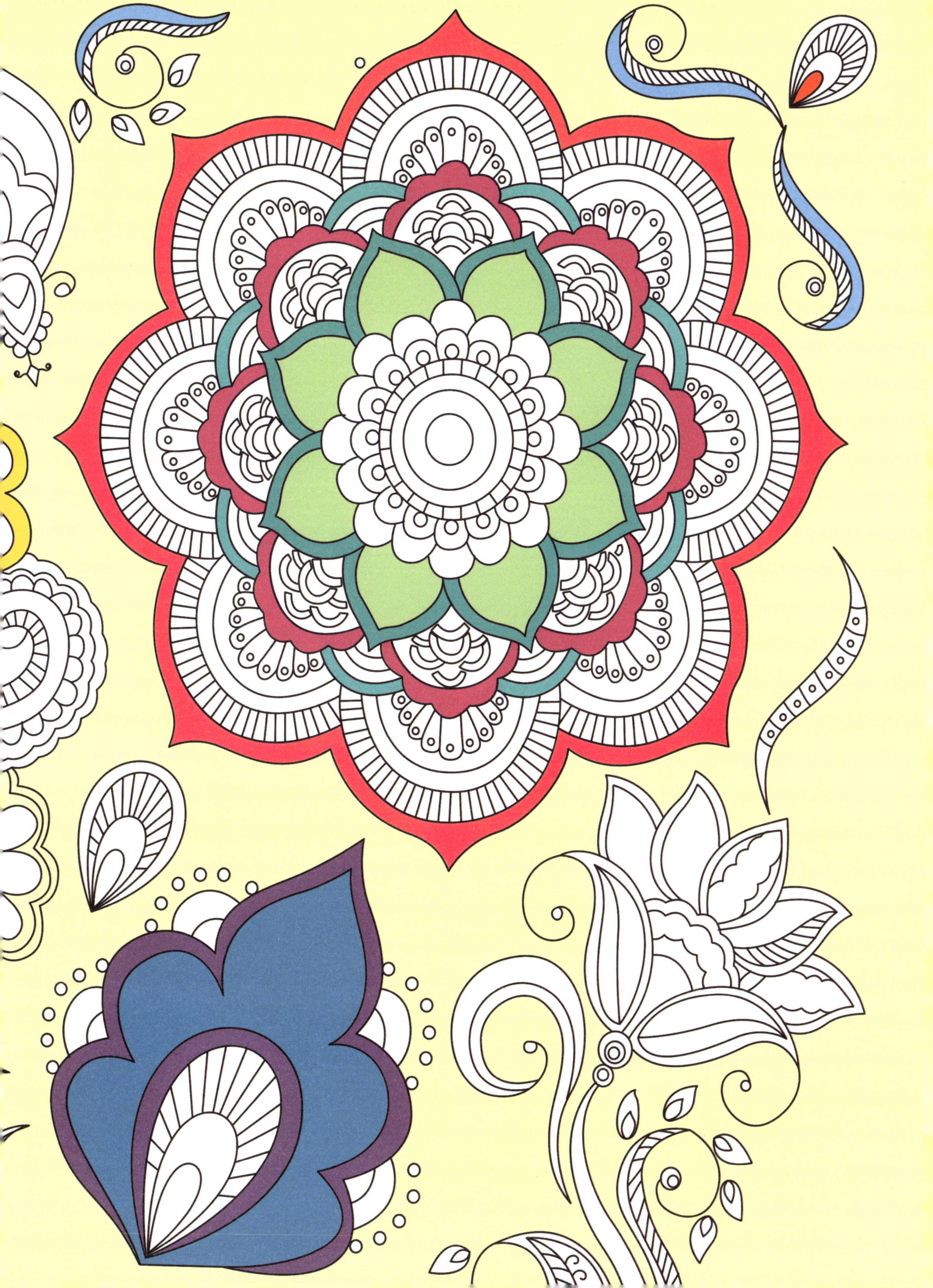

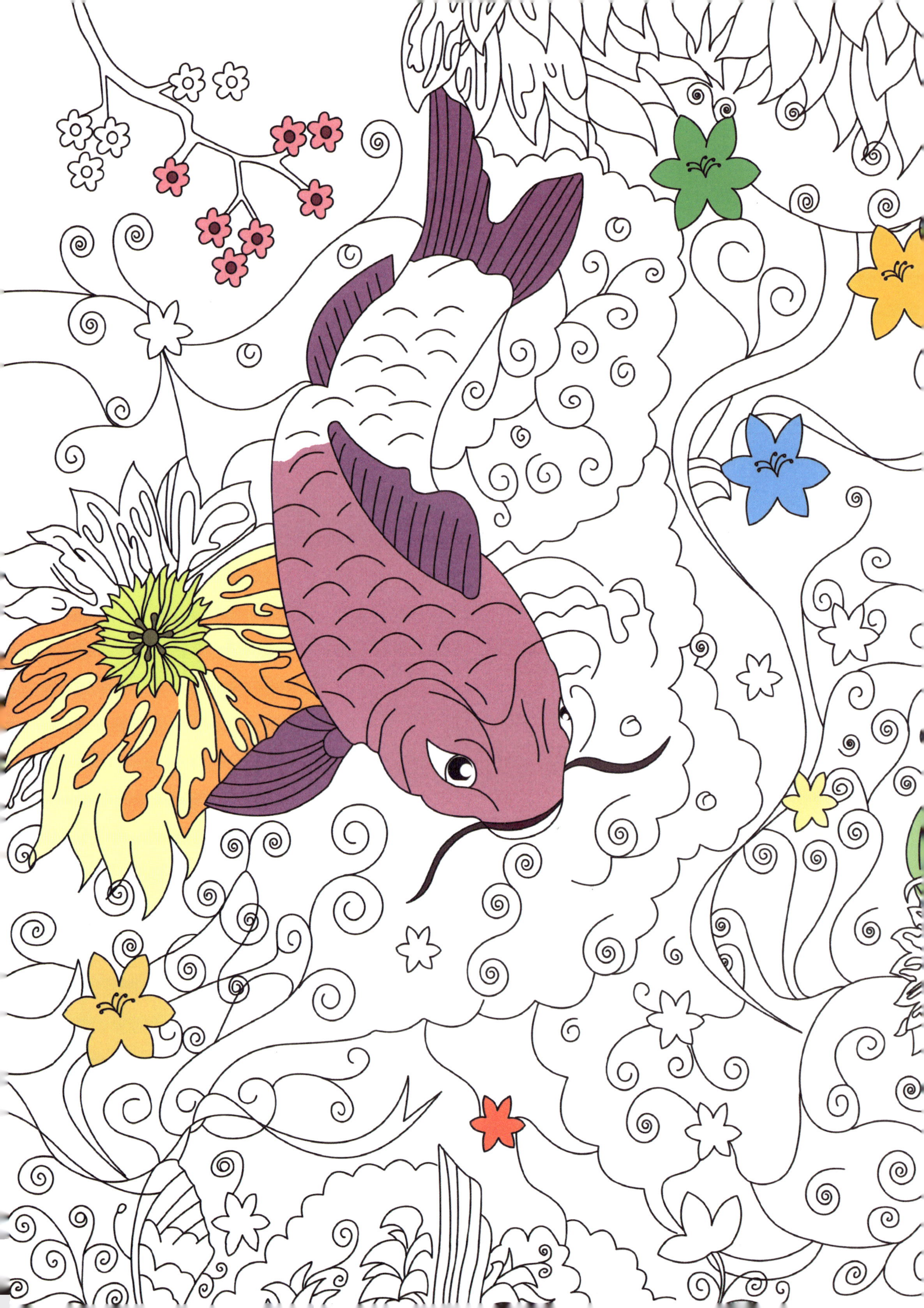

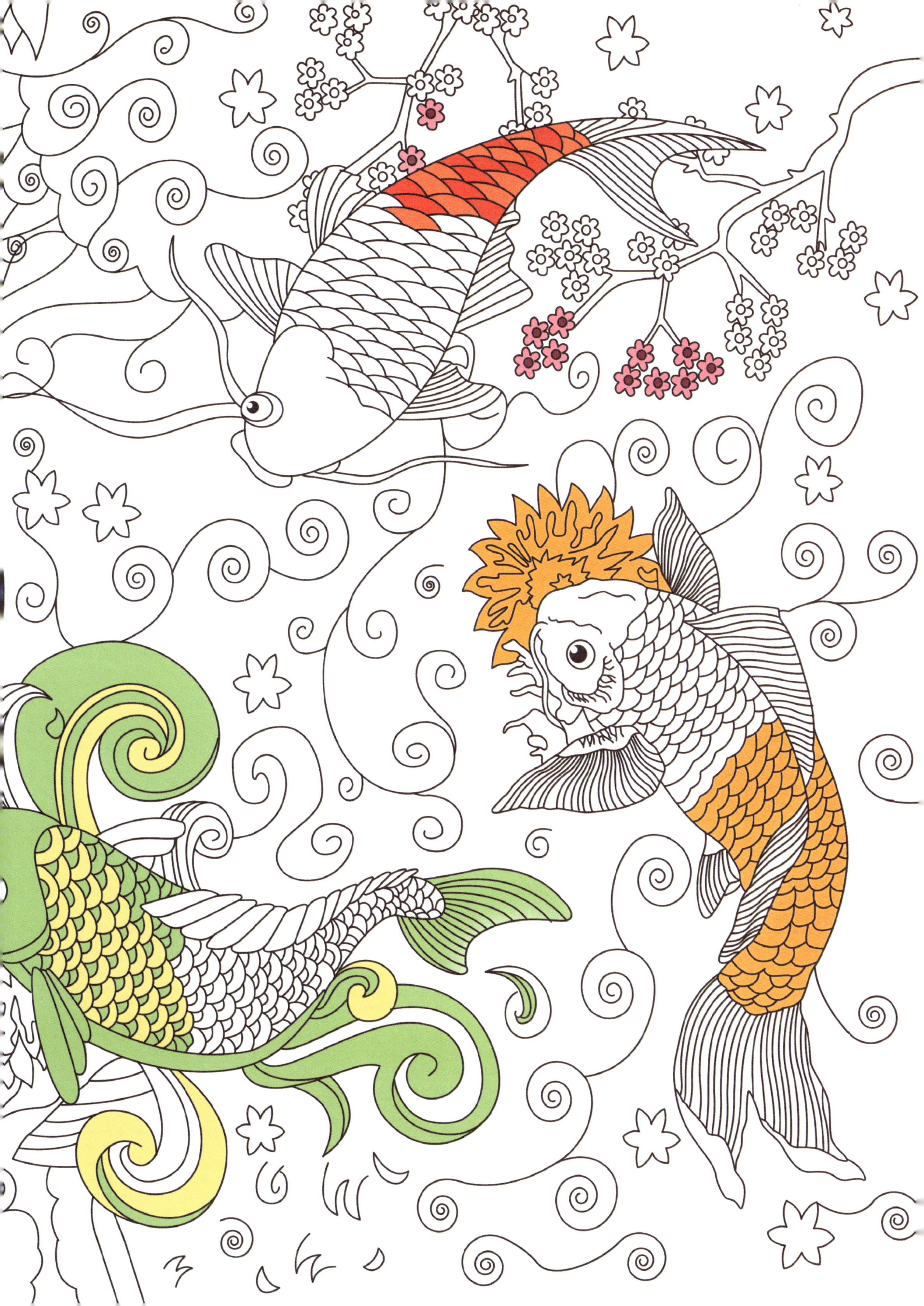

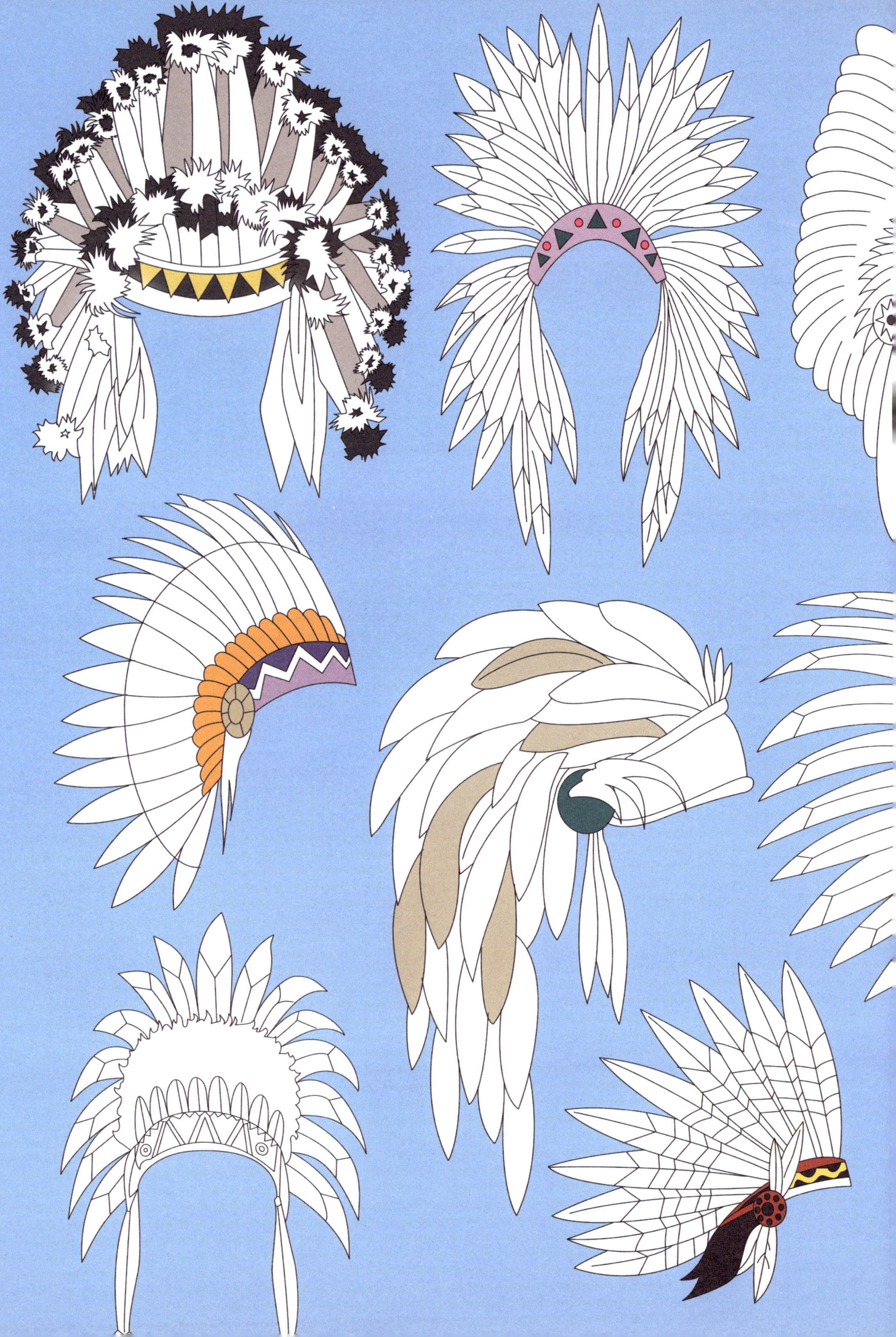

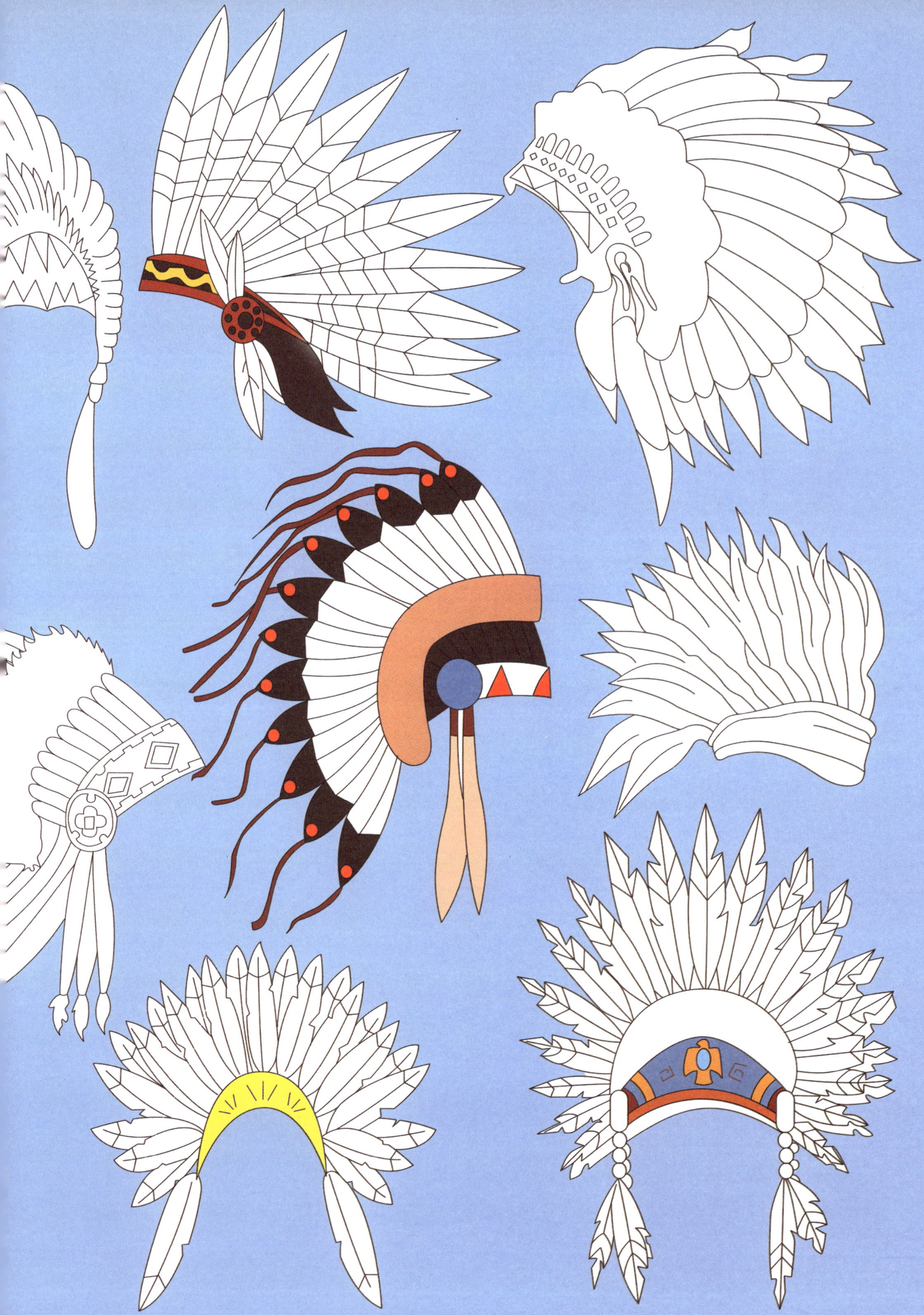

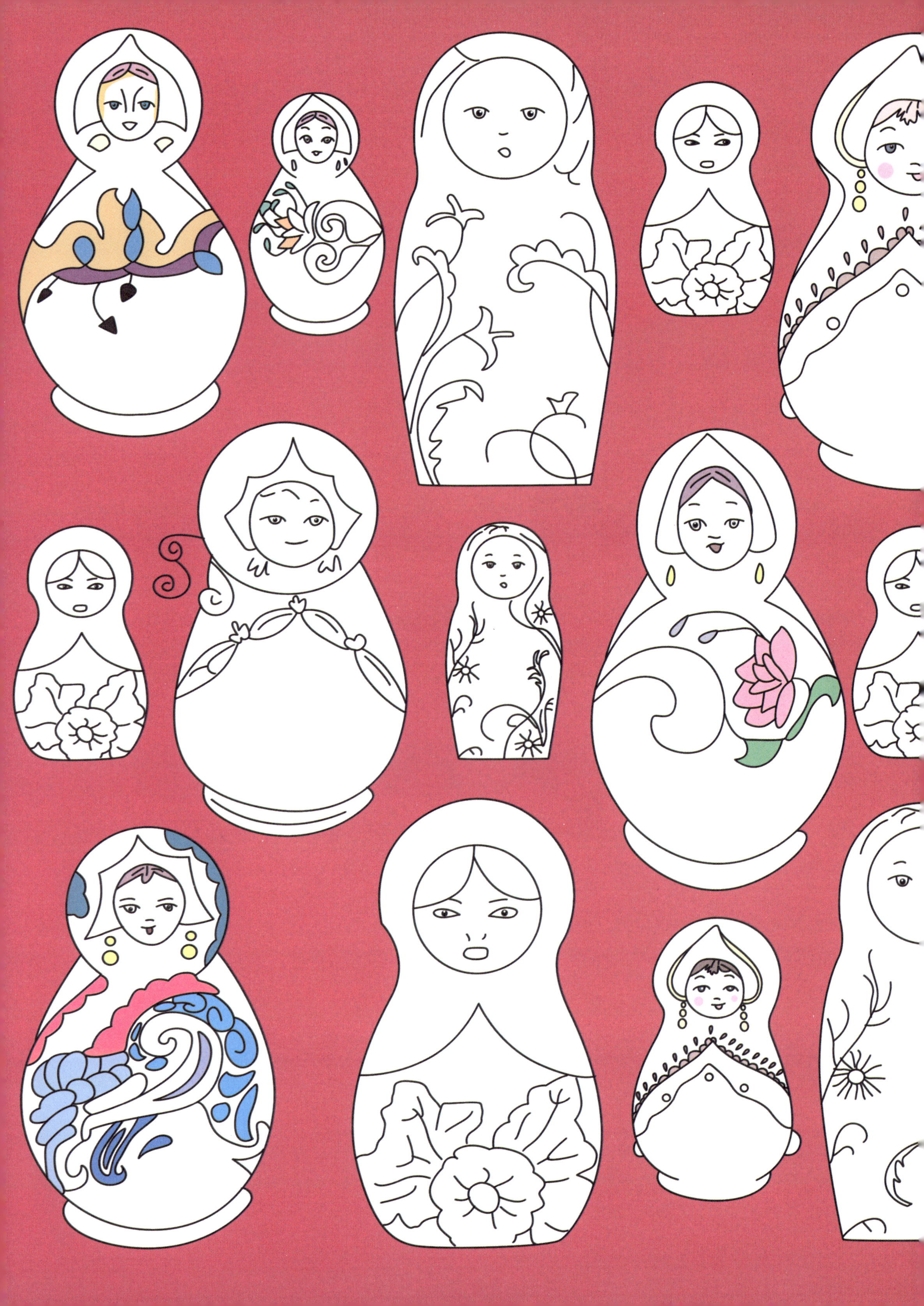

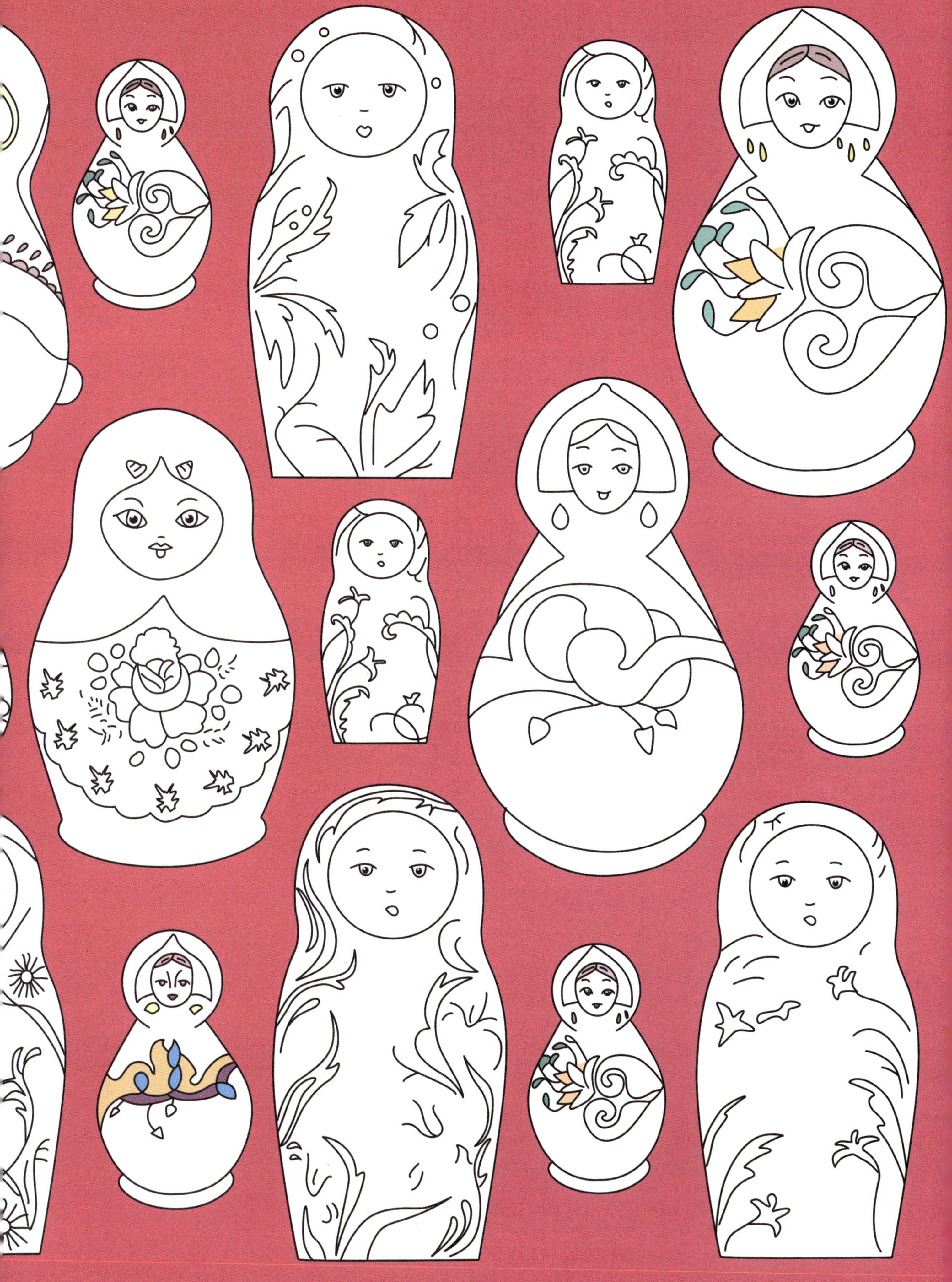

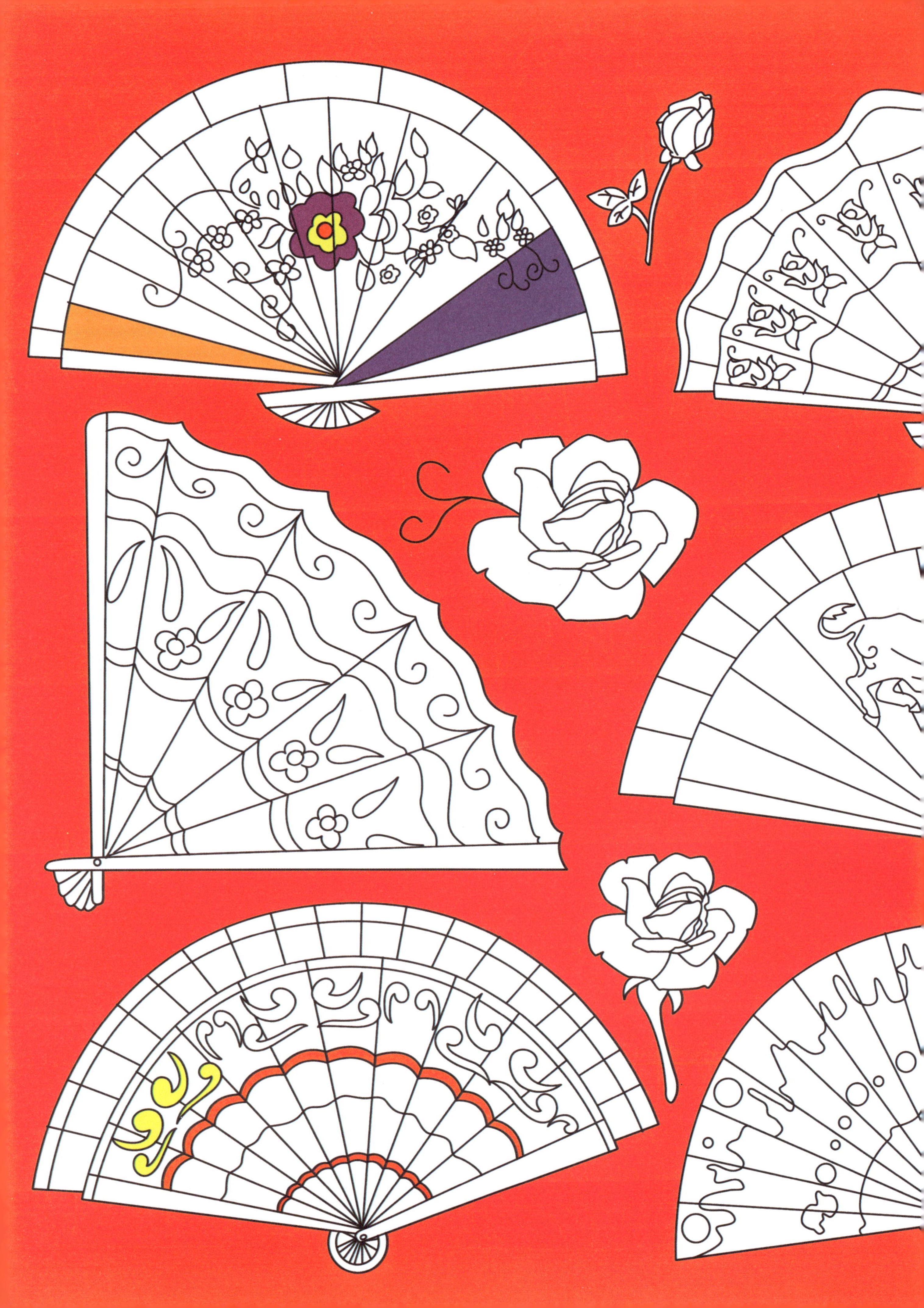

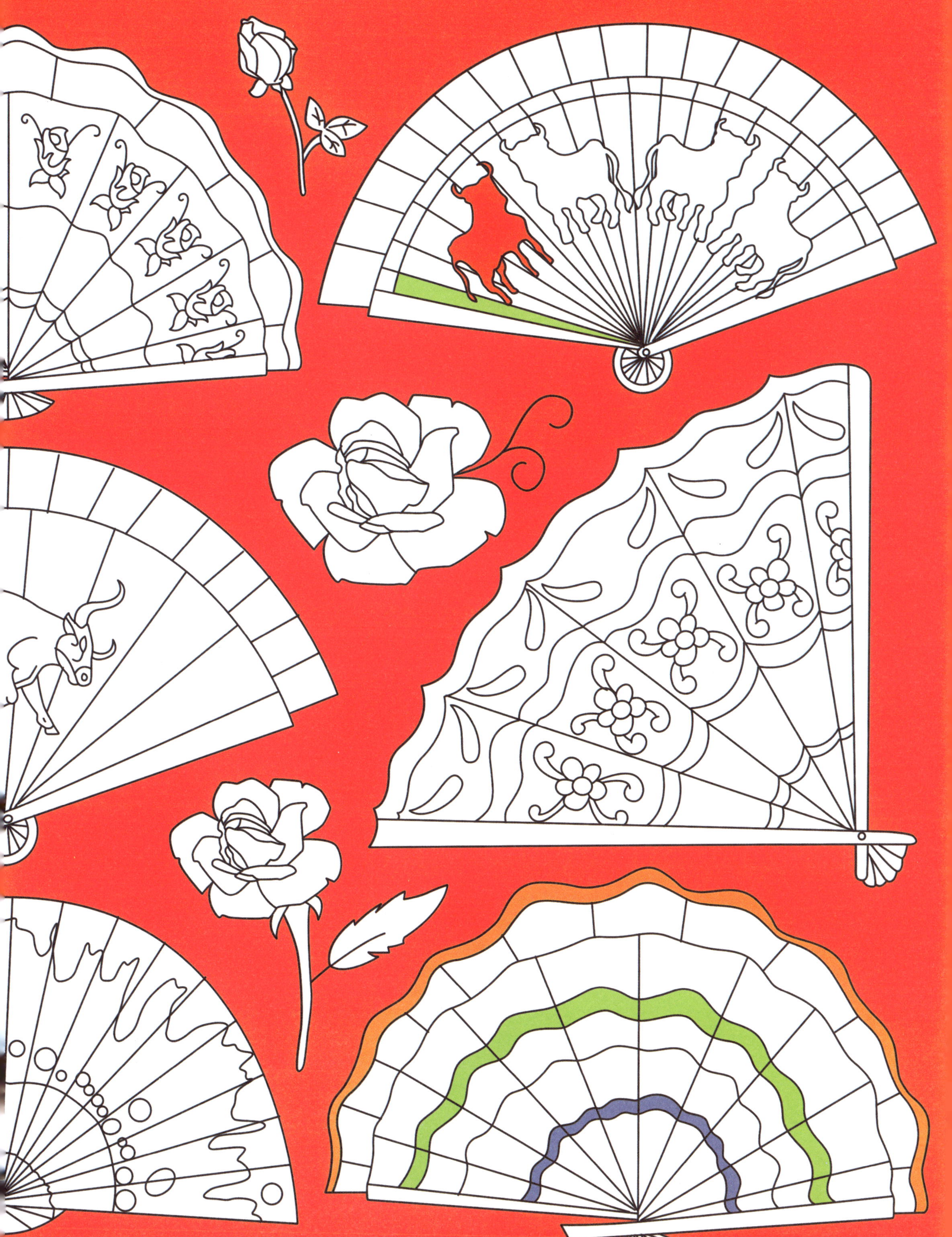

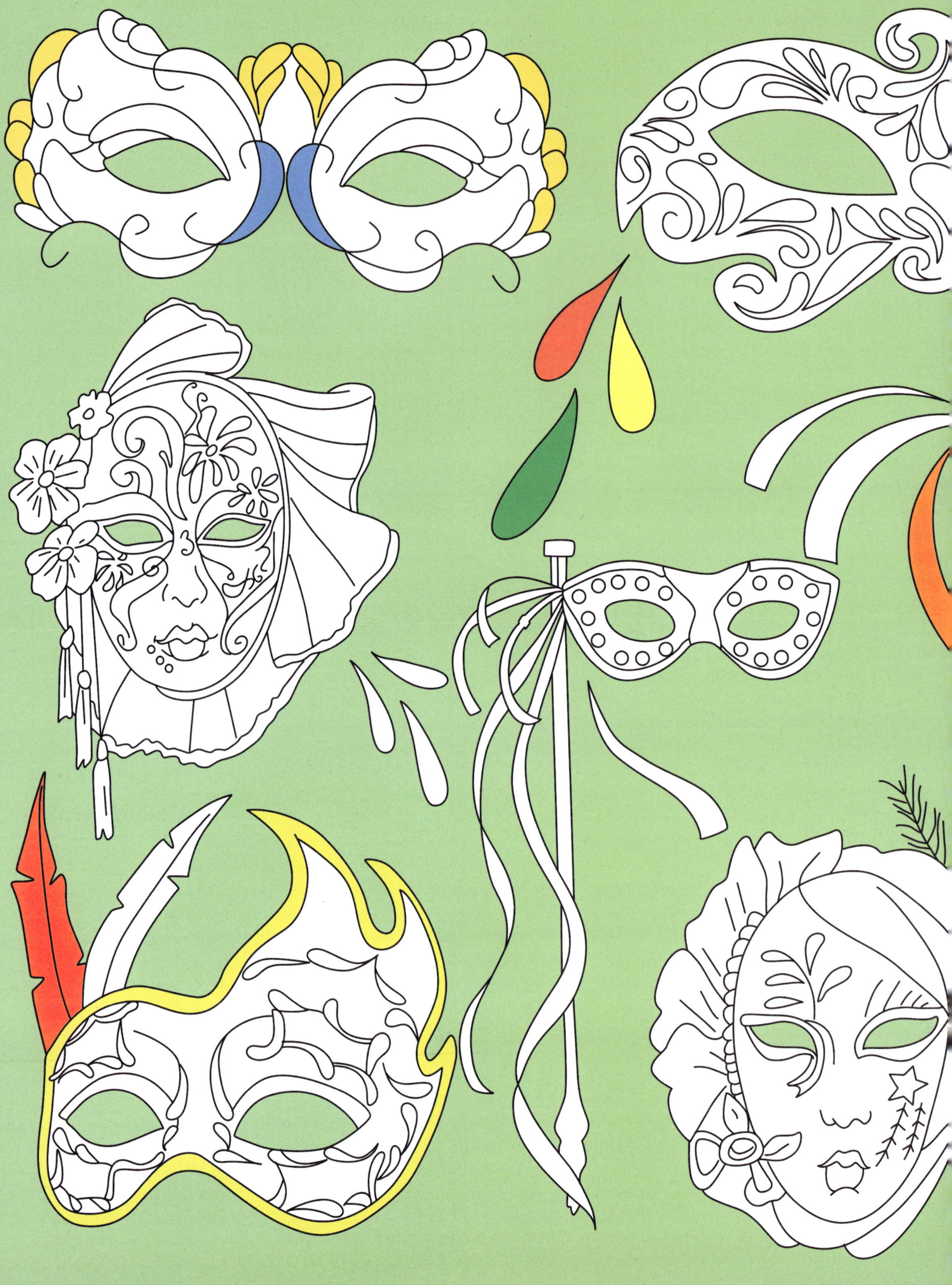

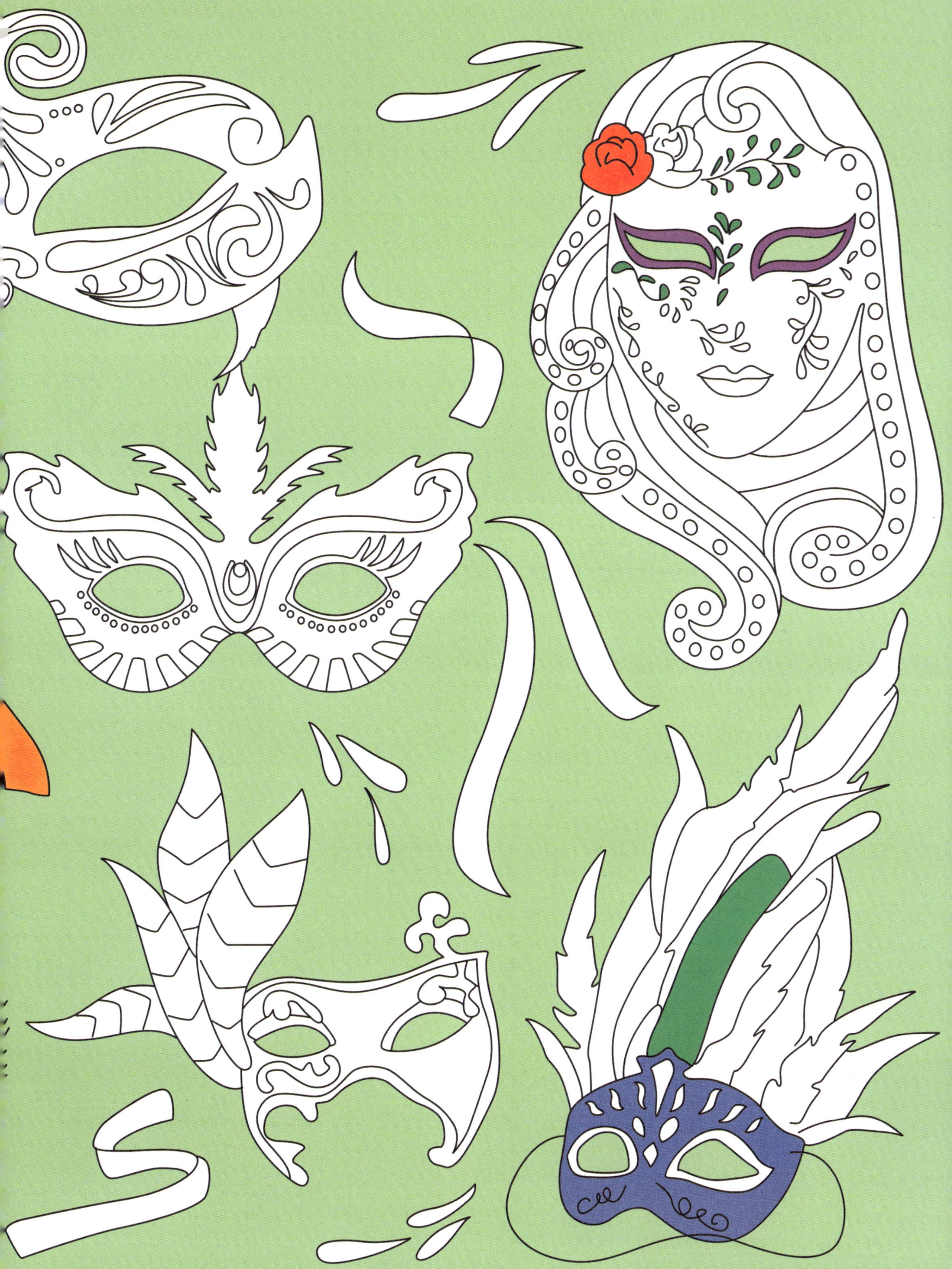

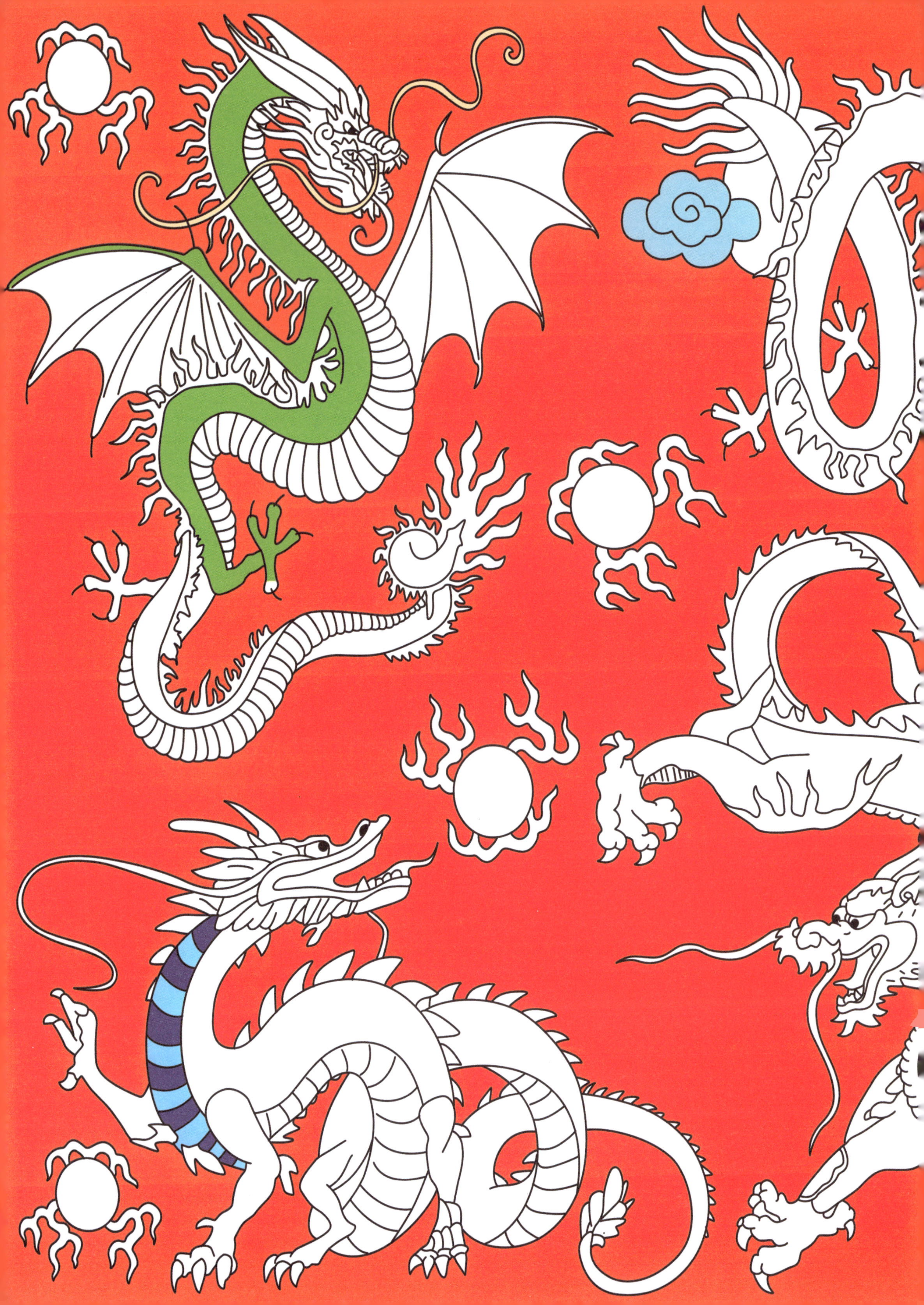

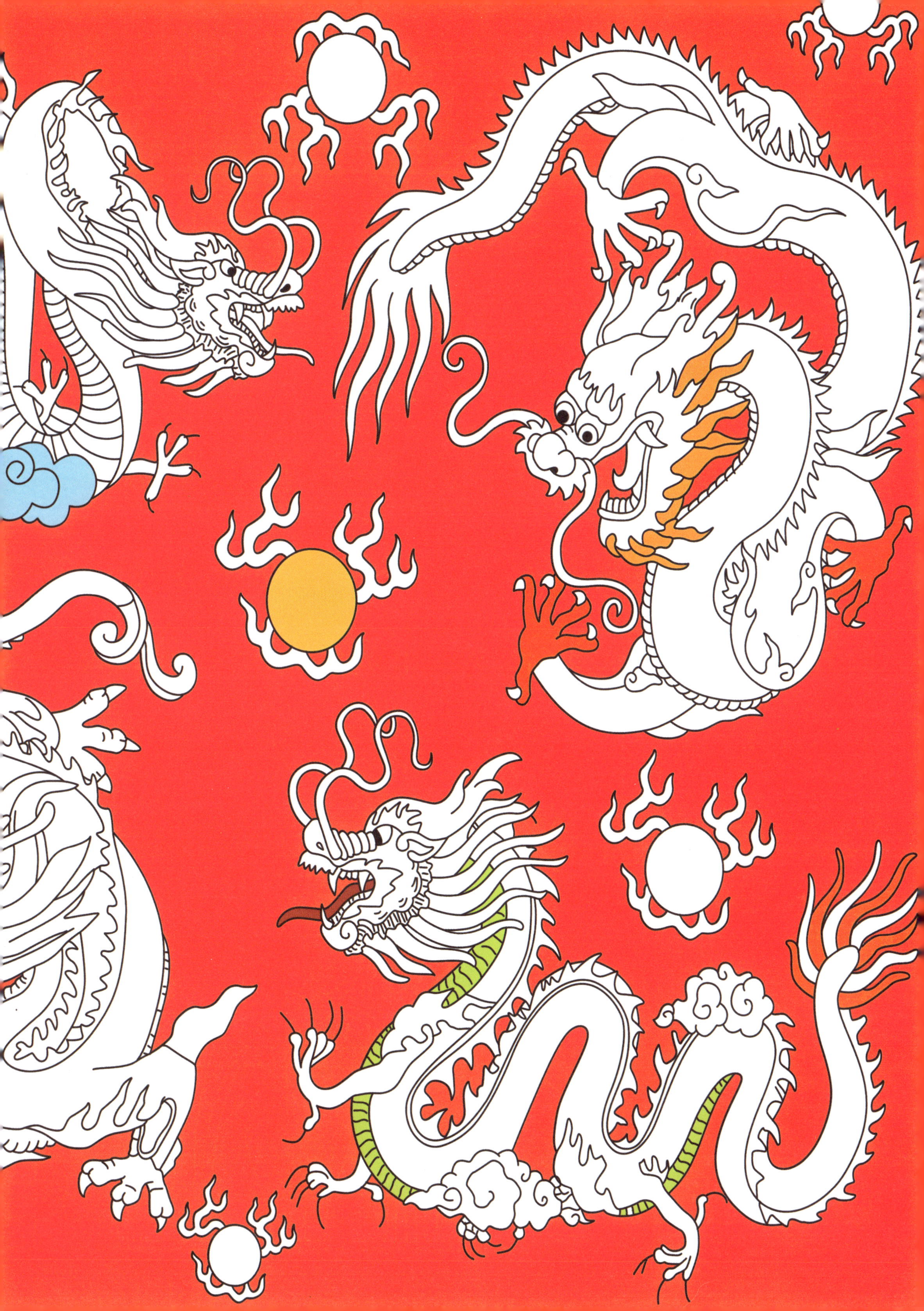

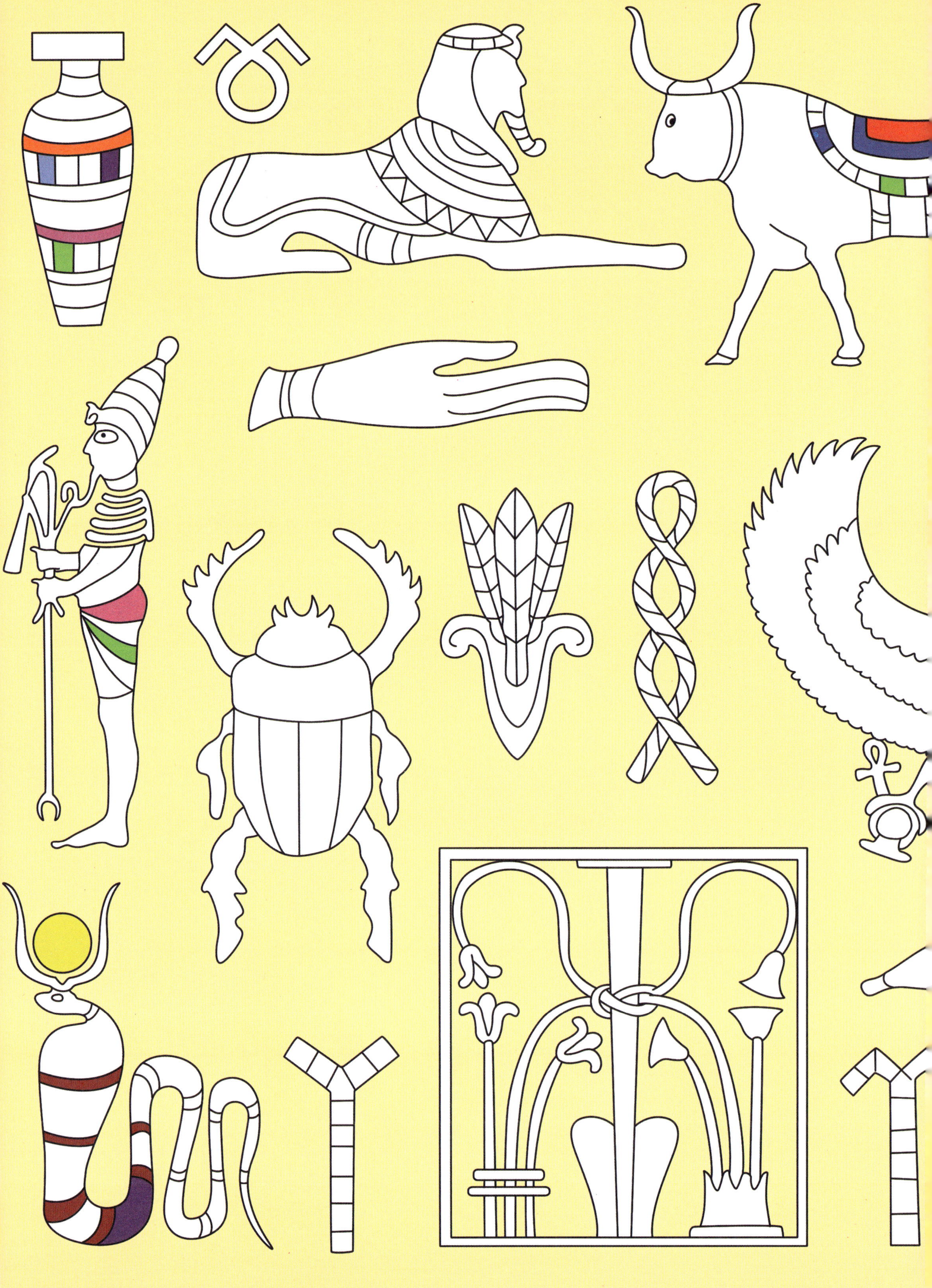

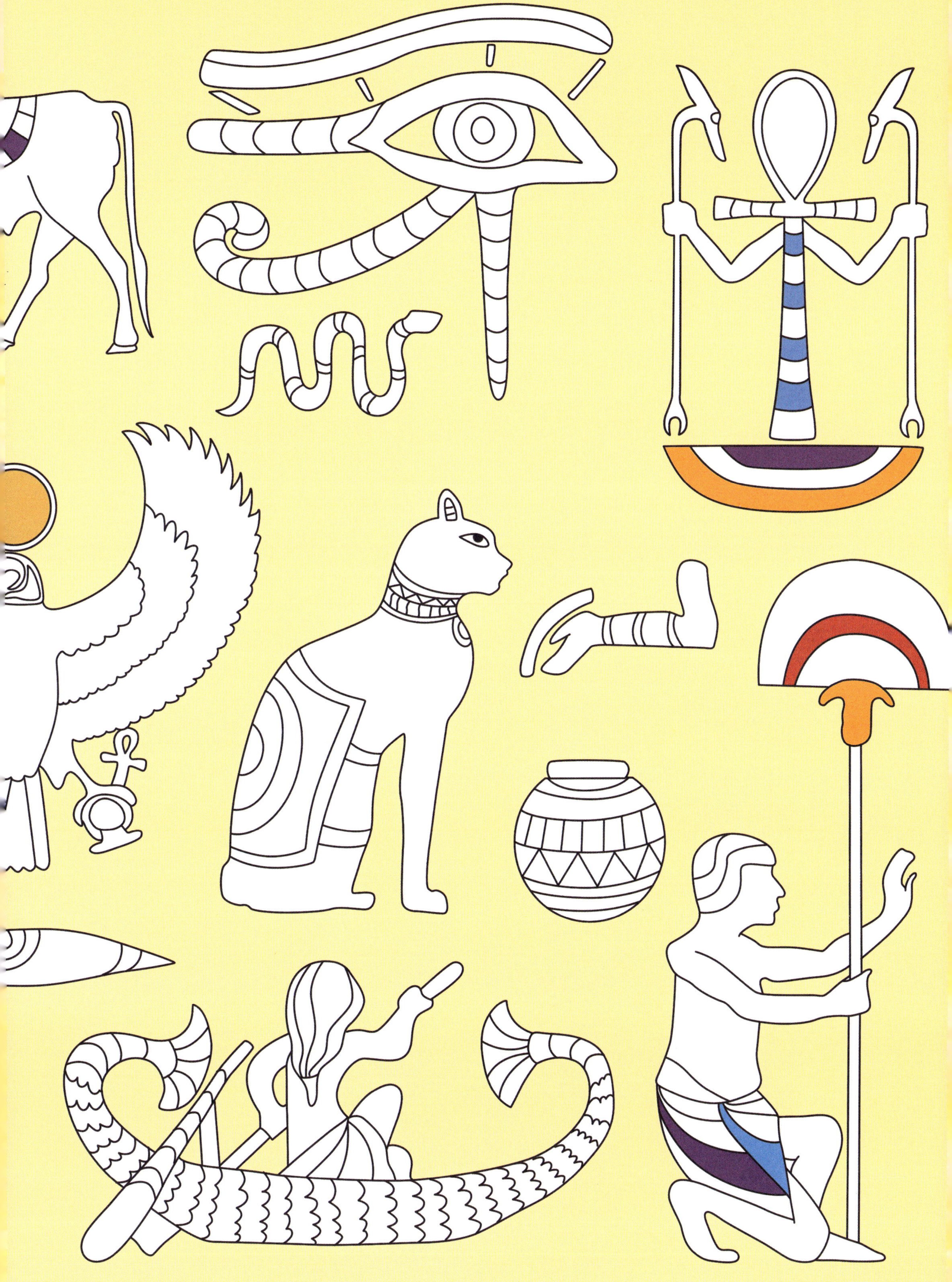

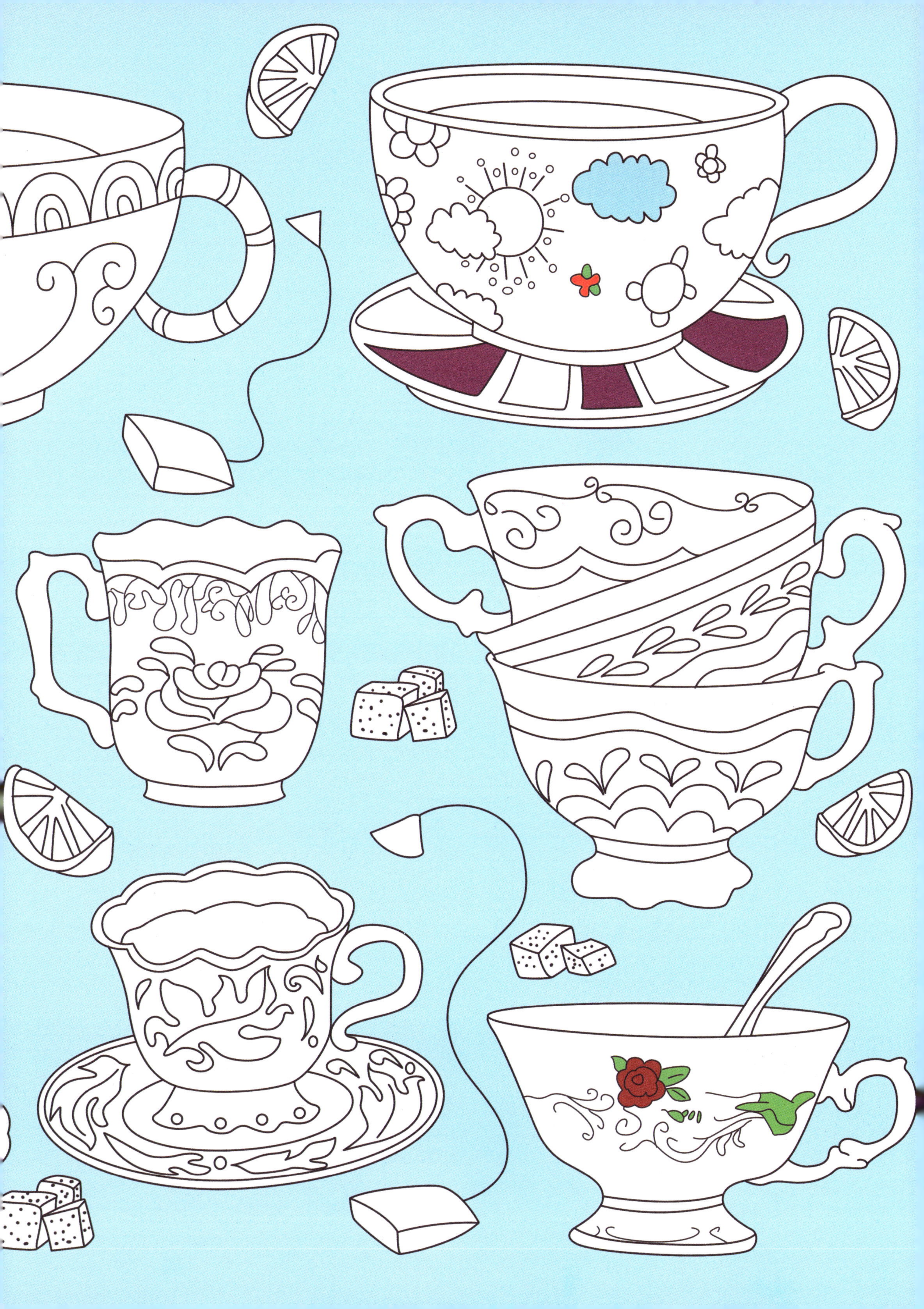

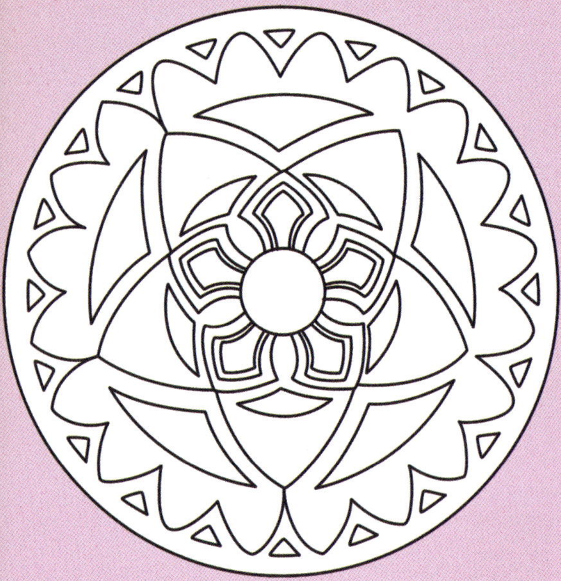
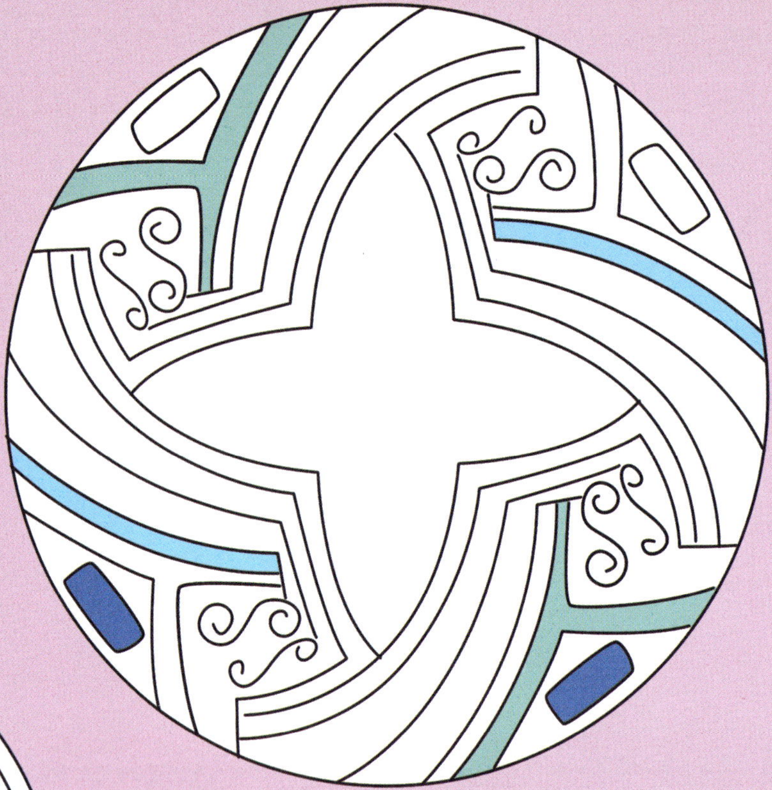
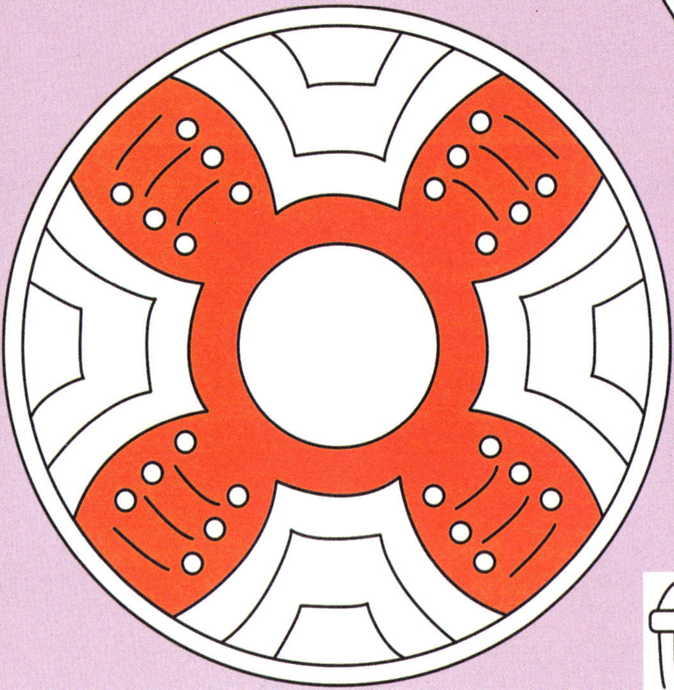
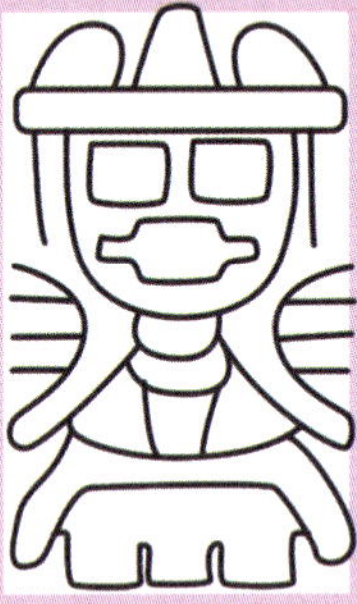
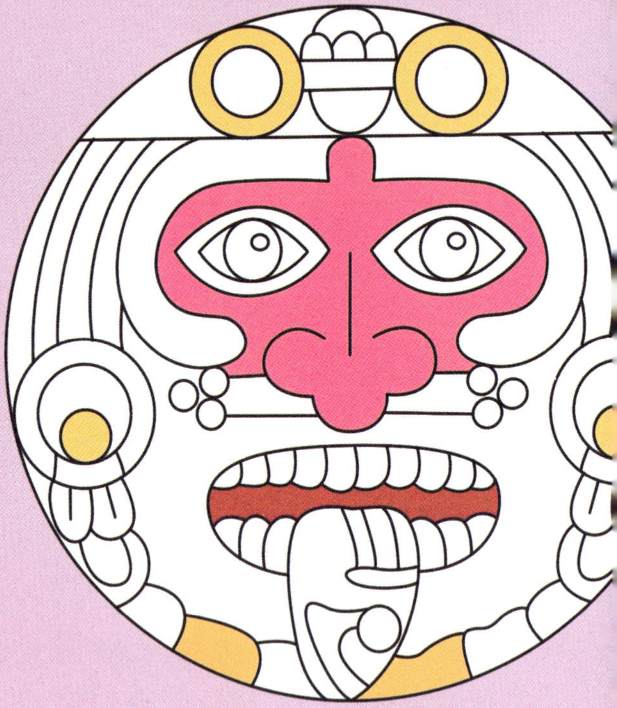

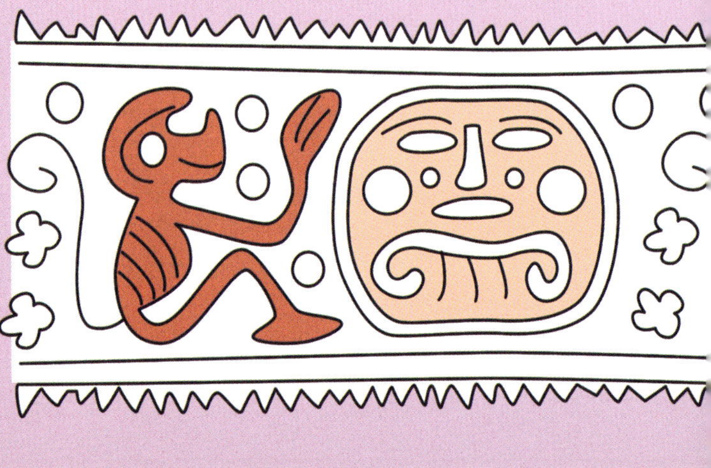

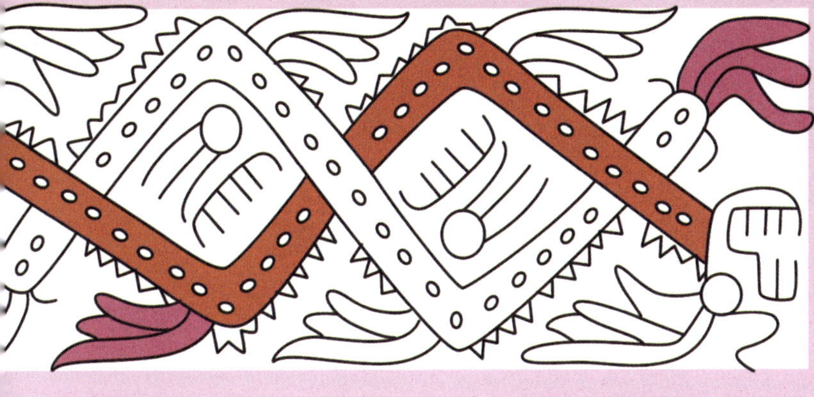
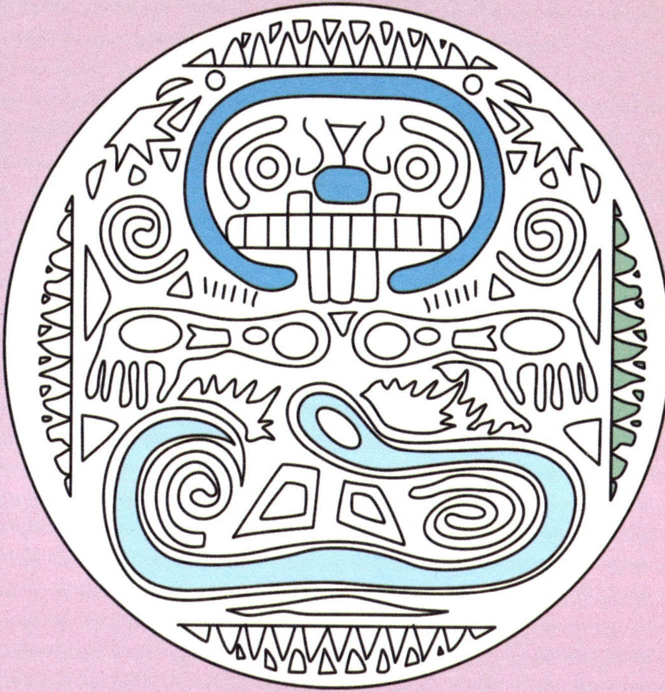
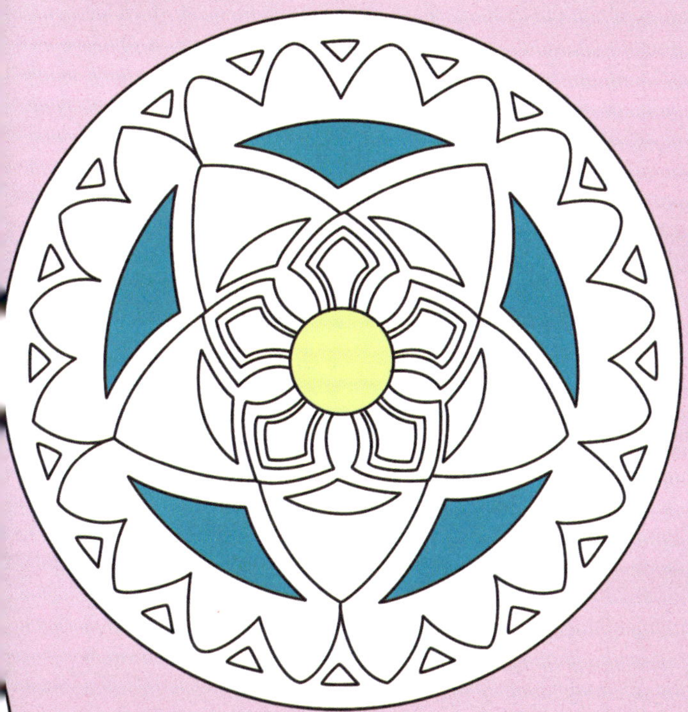
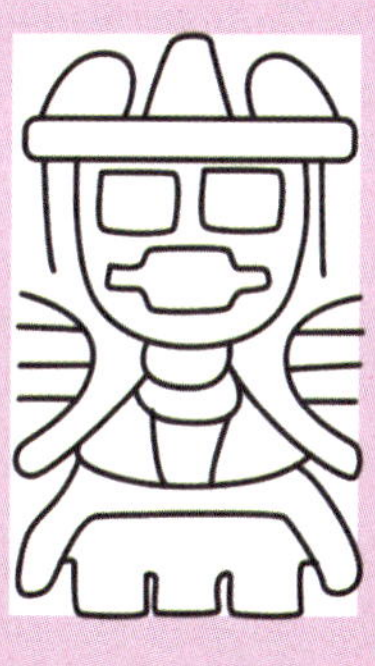
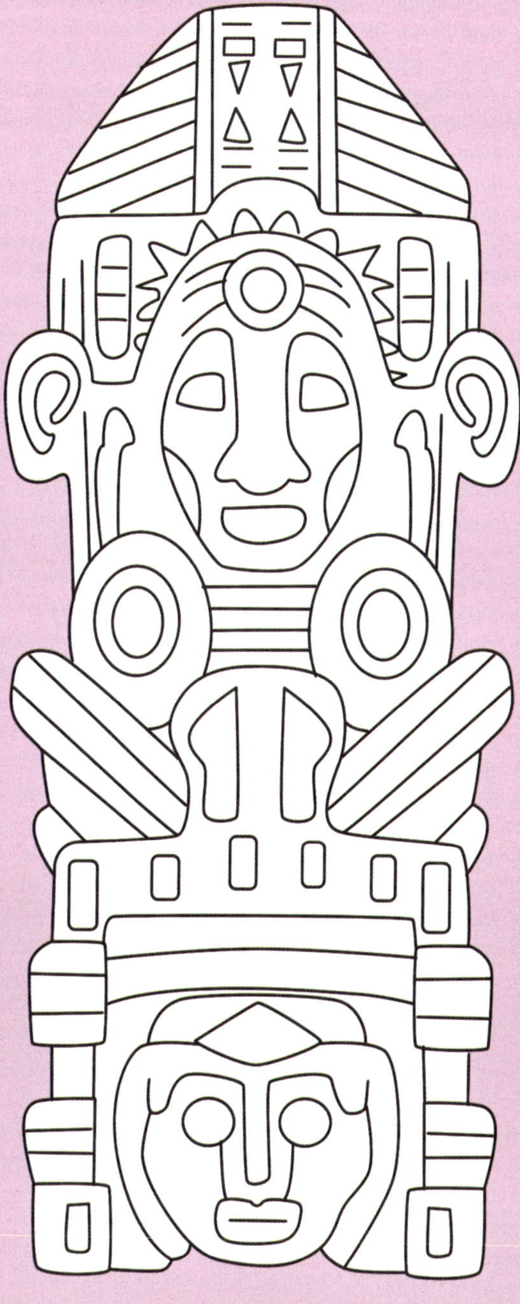
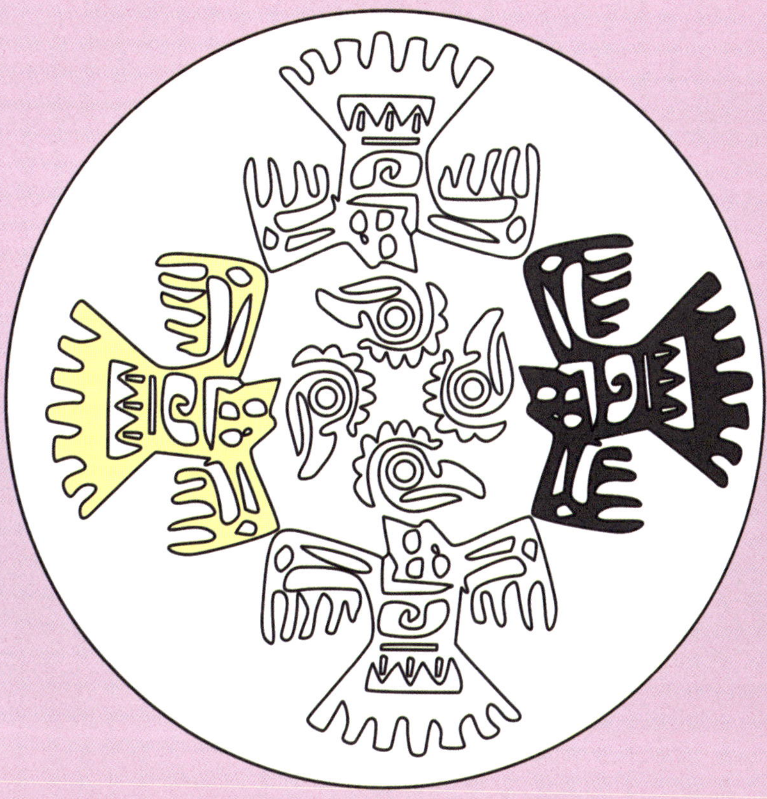
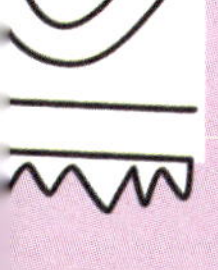

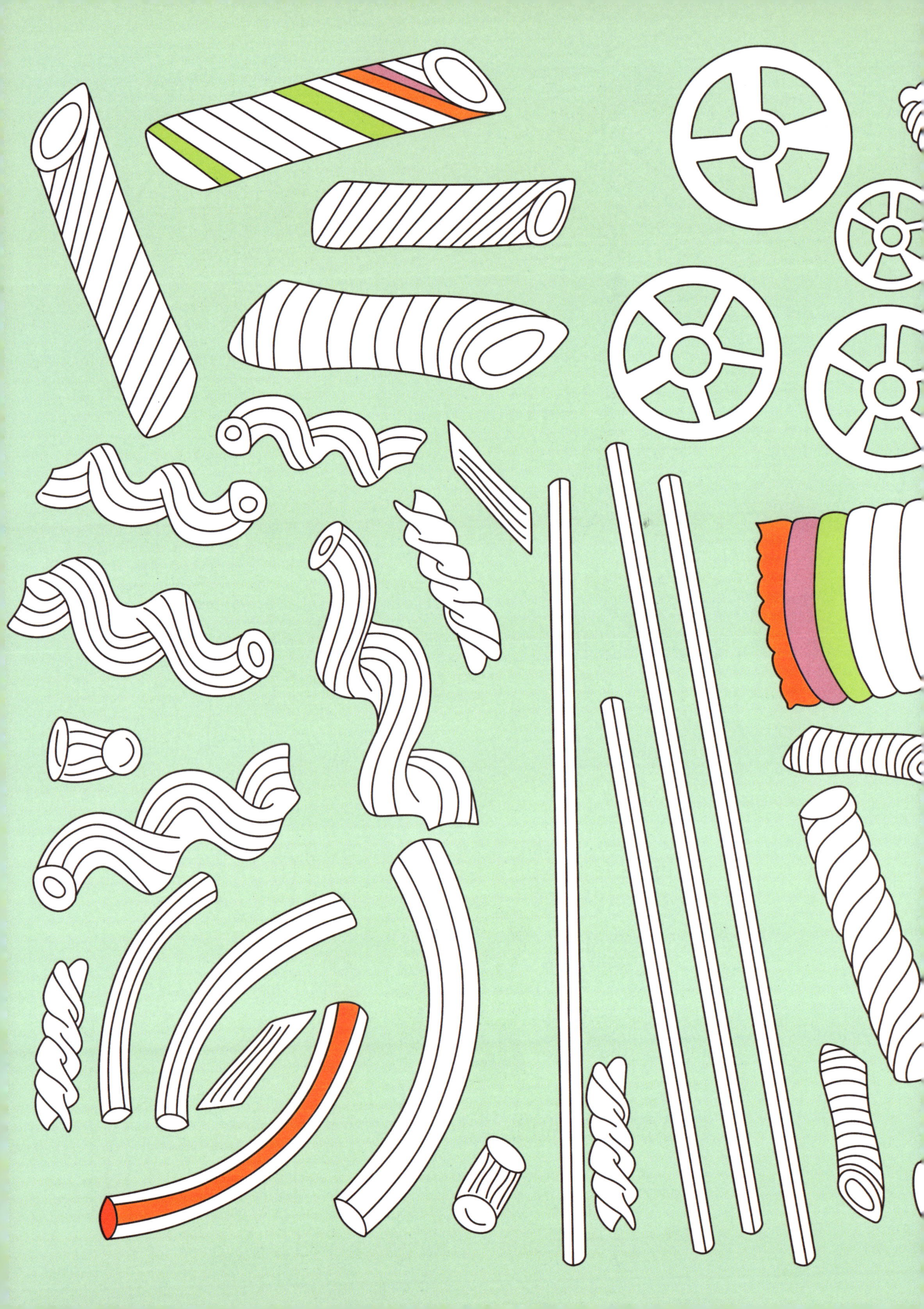

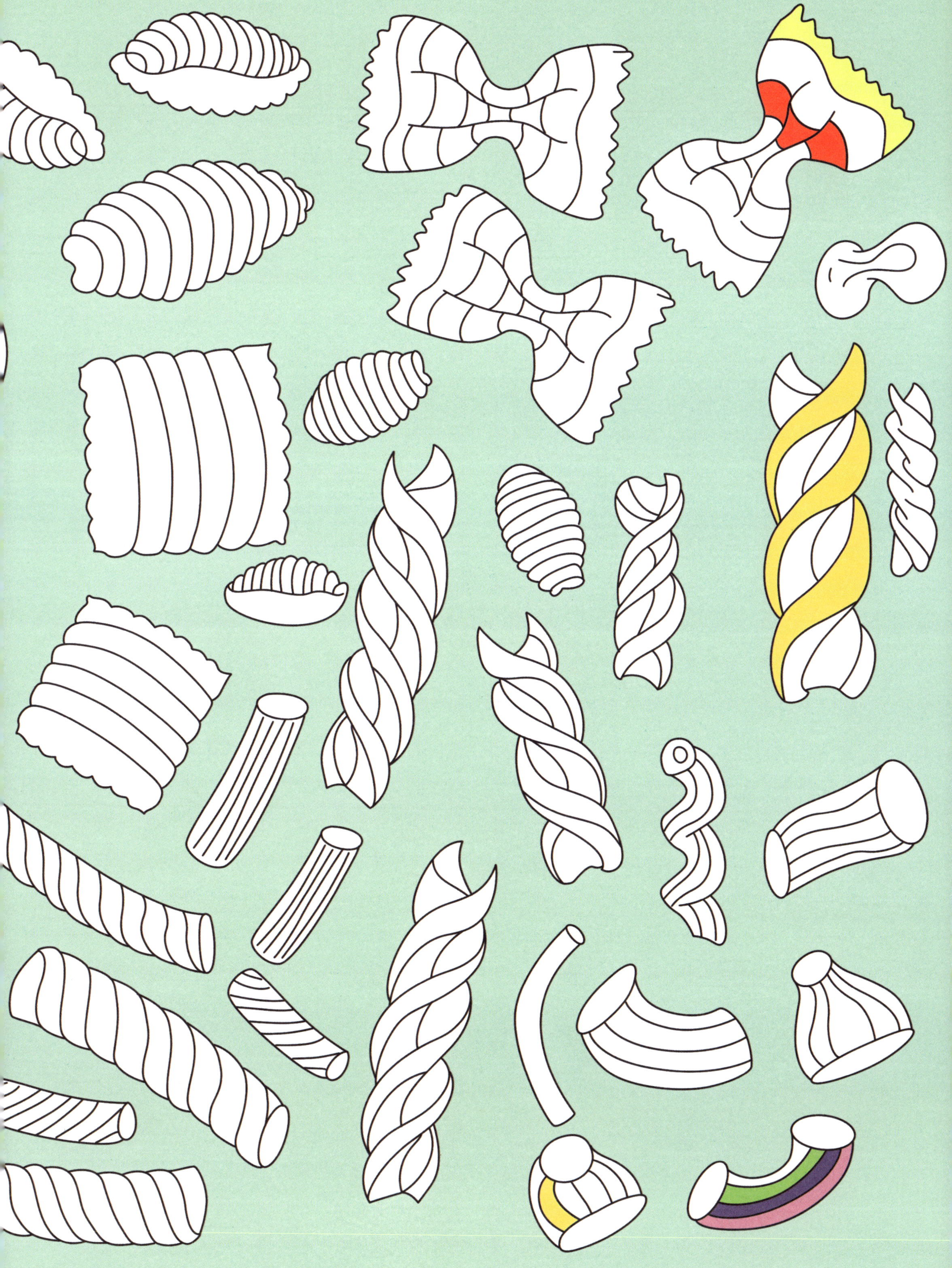

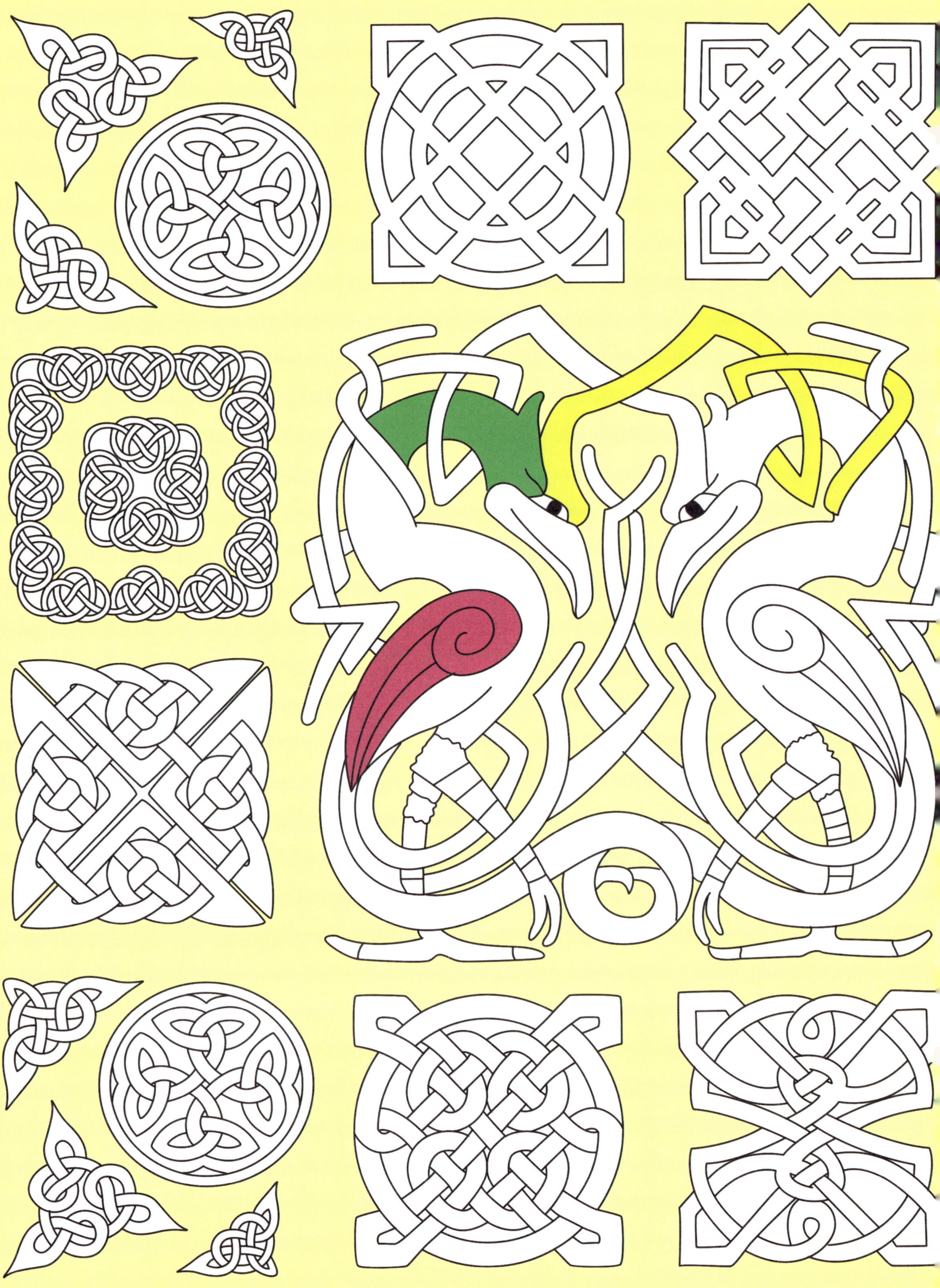

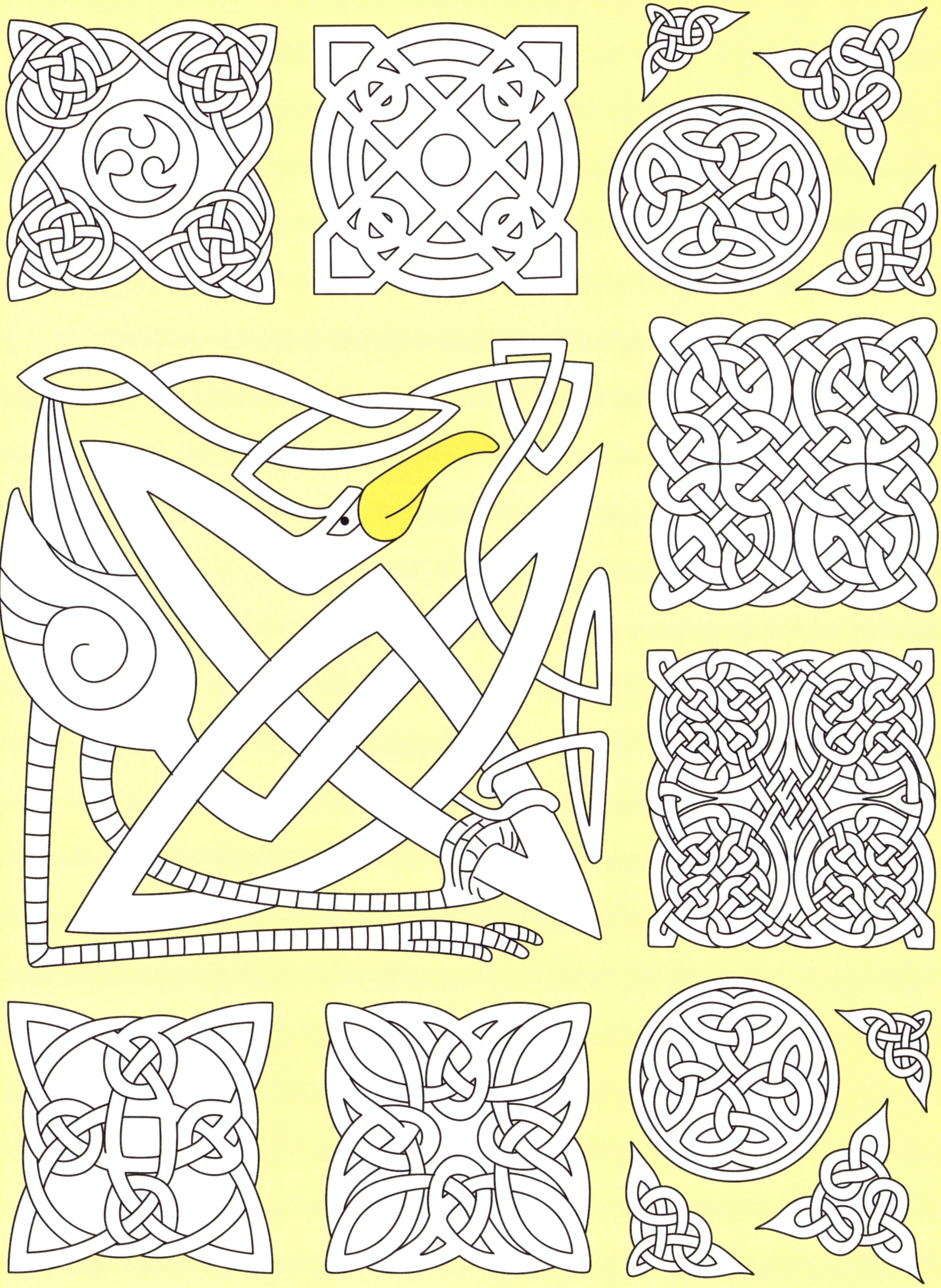

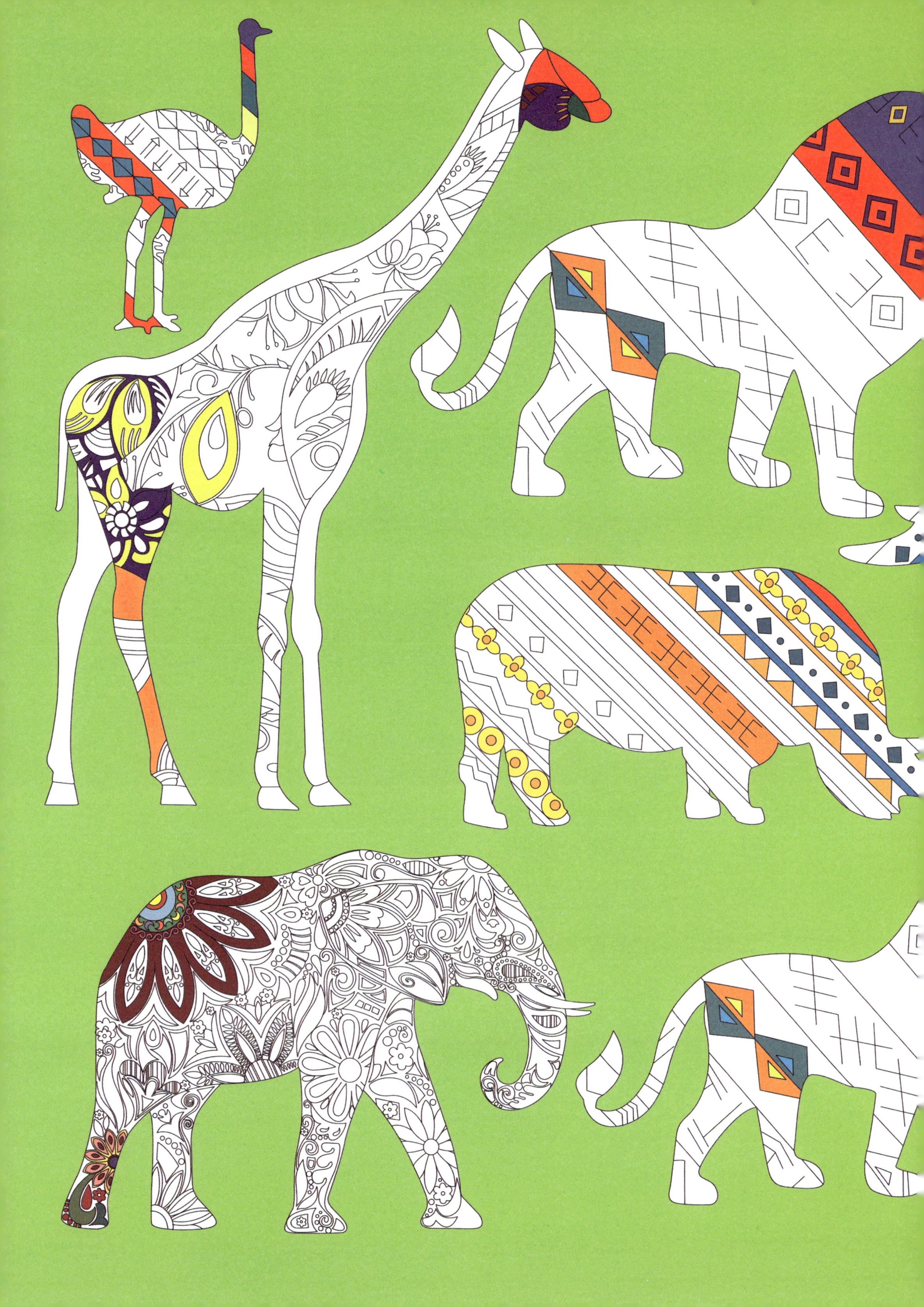

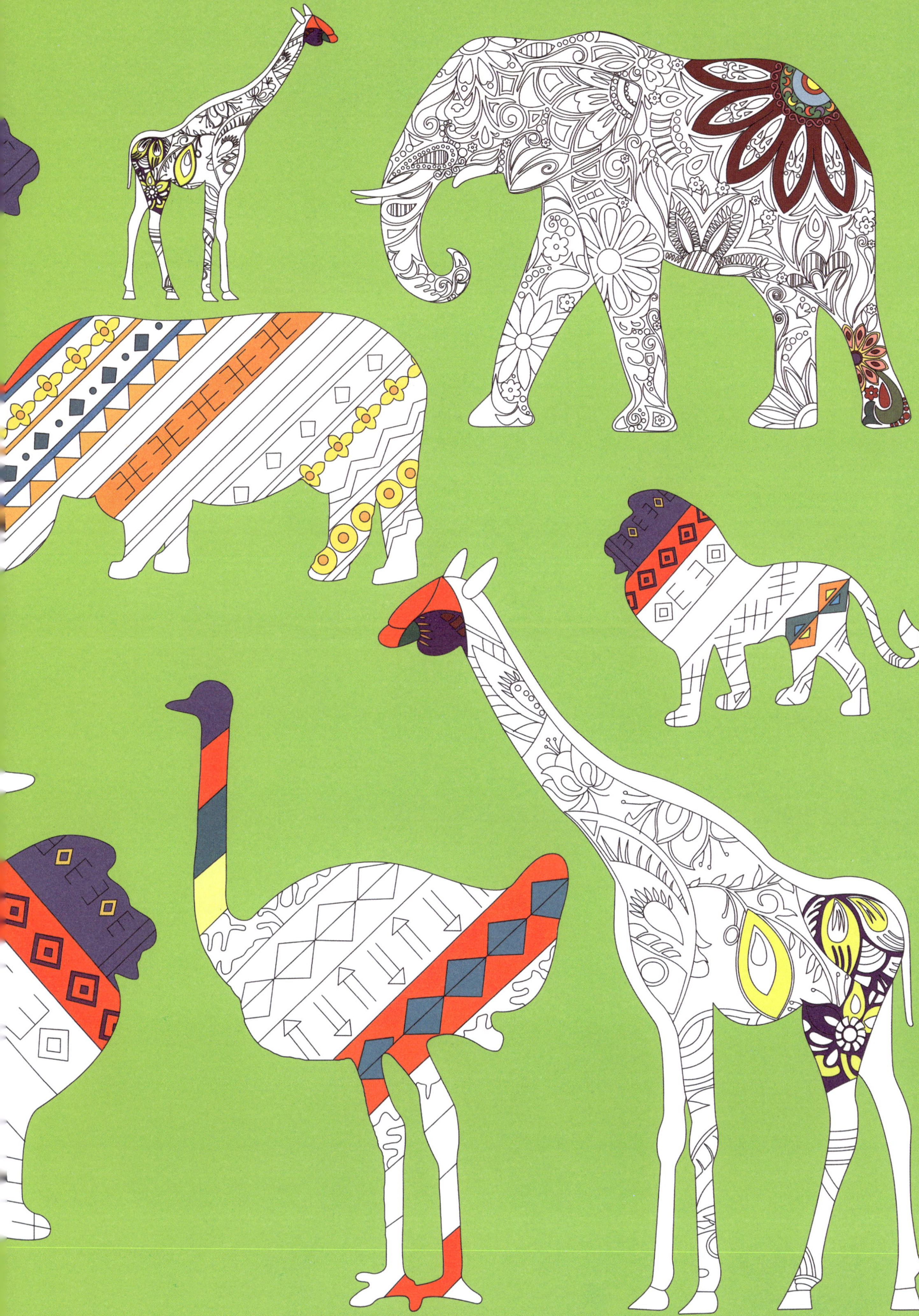

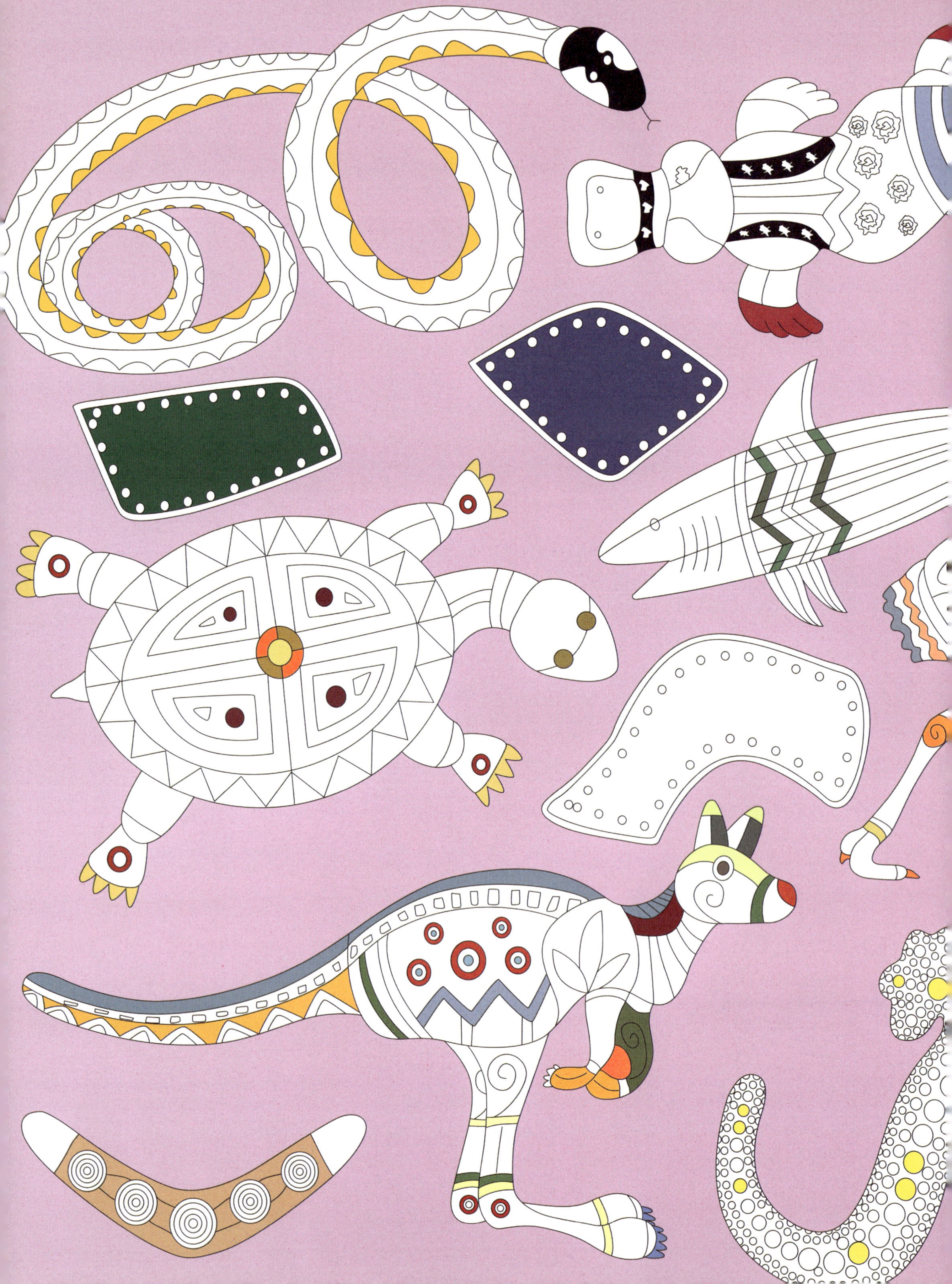

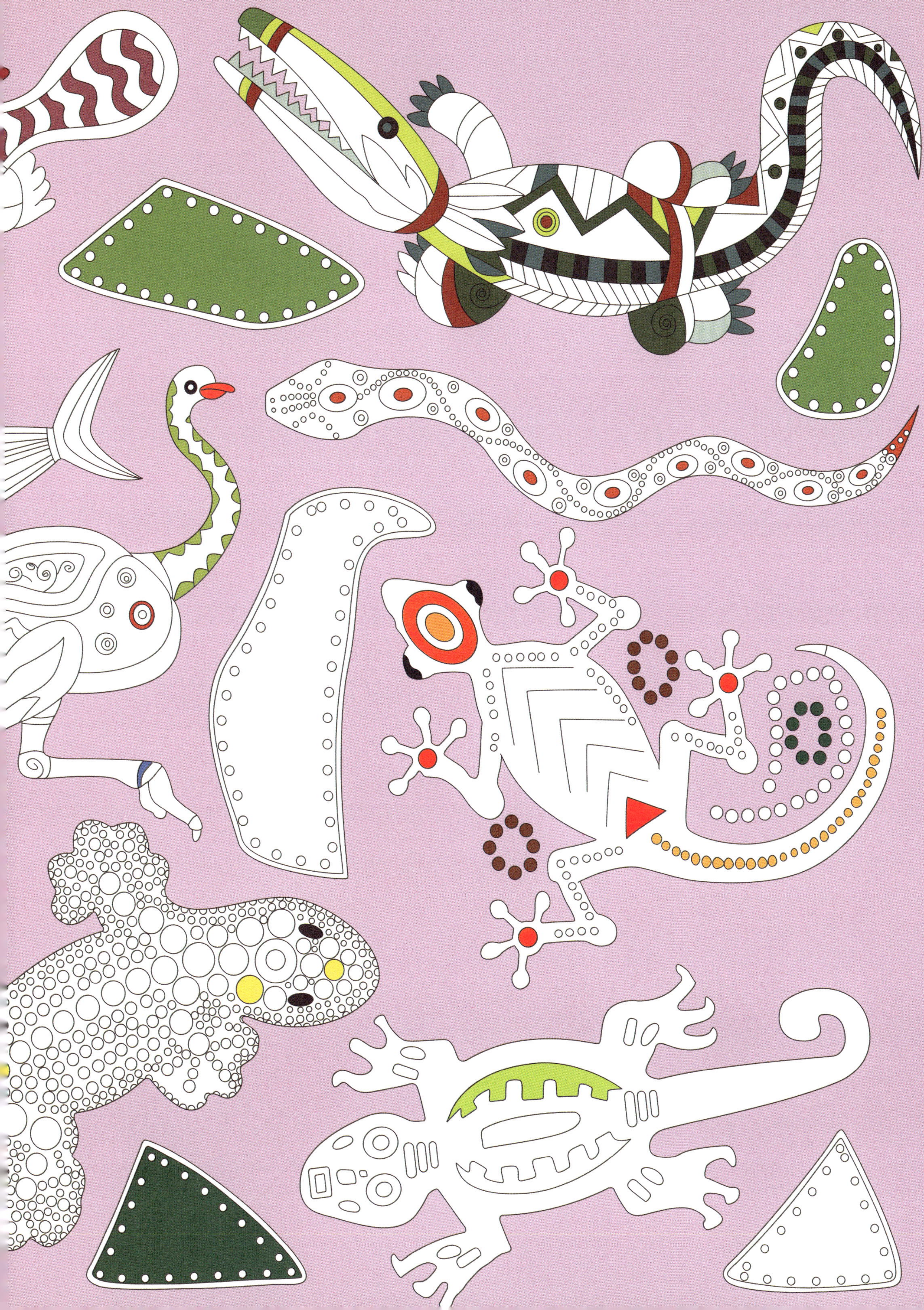

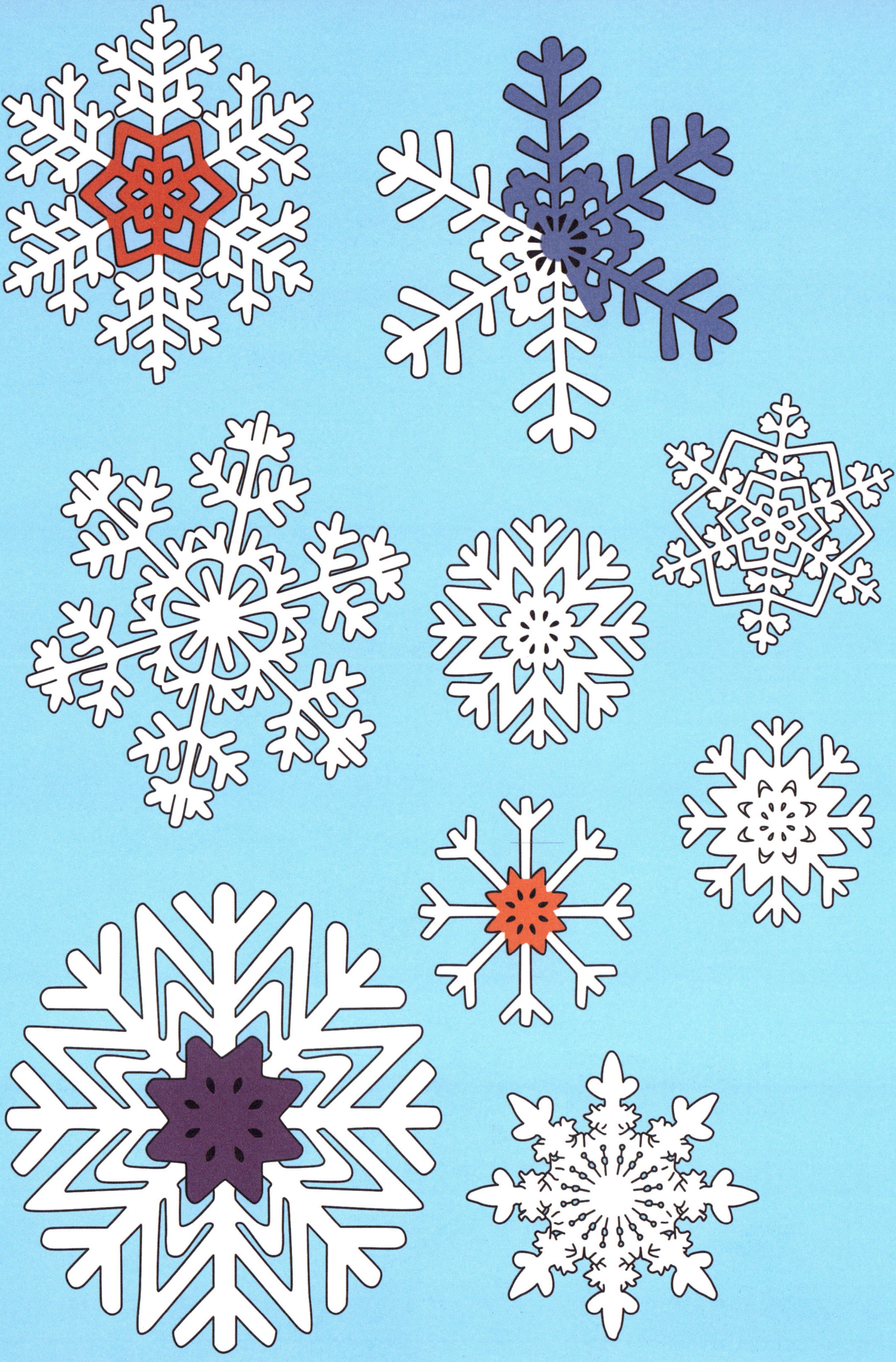